NOTES ON THE REVOLT

IN THE

NORTH-WESTERN PROVINCES OF INDIA

Owing to the antiquity and rarity of this book, certain pages are regrettably absent, and readability is compromised due to the blurring of the original text. If you possess any insights regarding the availability of these missing sections, kindly inform us. Your assistance is crucial in ensuring the completion of this significant work for the benefit of future generations.

NOTES ON THE REVOLT

IN THE

NORTH-WESTERN PROVINCES OF INDIA

CHARLES RAIKES

GYAN

Published by

Gyan Publishing House
5, Ansari Road
Daryaganj, New Delhi-110002
Phone: 011-47034999, 9811692060
E-mail: books@gyanbooks.com

Distribution Network
gyanbooks.com
India, USA, Canada, UK, Australia

ISBN: 978-93-6433-681-9 (HB)

First Published, 1858

2nd Impression 2024

Printed at: Gyan Press, Delhi.

NOTES ON THE REVOLT IN THE NORTH-WESTERN PROVINCES OF INDIA

Author: CHARLES RAIKES

NOTES ON THE REVOLT

IN THE

NORTH-WESTERN PROVINCES OF INDIA.

NOTES ON THE REVOLT

IN THE

NORTH-WESTERN PROVINCES OF INDIA.

BY

CHARLES RAIKES

JUDGE OF THE SUDDER COURT AT AGRA:

LATE CIVIL COMMISSIONER WITH SIR COLIN CAMPBELL:

AUTHOR OF "NOTES ON THE NORTH-WESTERN PROVINCES OF INDIA."

LONDON

LONGMAN, BROWN, GREEN, LONGMANS, & ROBERTS.

1858

PREFACE.

THE Author of the following Notes has only very recently returned from India. He has observed the anxiety on the part of the educated portion of his countrymen to acquire authentic information as to the present feelings and past conduct of the people of India; and has thought it right to place before the public an account, however hurried and imperfect, of his observations during the past year.

Having no personal adventures to recount, the writer's apology for relating his own history is his desire to support the opinions advanced in the concluding chapters of this book. For it is only from a recital of facts that we can gather material for our future conduct; and in these days any honest narrator of the Indian history of his day may hope for the indulgence of the public.

London: July, 1858.

CONTENTS.

NOTES ON THE REVOLT

&c.

CHAPTER I.

THE FIRST OUTBREAK.

On the morning of the 11th May, 1857, I was seated in my library at Agra, quietly preparing for the labour of the day, when a slip of paper was placed on my table. I read as follows:—

"*The Mofussilite Extra.*

"Agra, Monday, May 11, 1857.

"A telegraphic message from Meerut* states that the troopers of the 3rd Cavalry have mutinied, setting fire to their own lines and several officers' bungalows, killing and wounding all European

* Meerut is 131 miles north-west from Agra. There is a good cross road from Agra to Allygurh on the Grand Trunk road. The distance from Agra to Allygurh is 51 miles, and from Allygurh to Meerut, 80 miles. This telegraphic message was a private one, sent to some resident of Agra, who was about to start for Meerut, and was thus saved from probable destruction.

officers and soldiers they could find near their lines.

"In a station like Meerut, with the 6th Dragoons, 60th Rifles, and European artillery, it may be presumed that the mutineers had a very short race of it. Further particulars have been sent for.

"The Calcutta Government Gazette announces the disbanding of seven companies of the 34th Native Infantry.

"Letters from Meerut state that the eighty-five troopers 3rd Cavalry have been tried. Those most to blame have been sentenced to ten years' imprisonment, others to five years.

I felt, as may be supposed, the gravity of the event thus suddenly announced. It was the bursting of the thunder-cloud I had been long and anxiously watching; or rather, the mine so long charged had at last been sprung. The fabric of the Bengal army was tottering to ruin; to pull down with it the civil and political institutions which that army had for a hundred years supported.

At noon the judges of the Sudder Court assembled as usual. Business went on according to rule. Cases were tried, pleadings heard, and decrees passed. But the mind of the European functionaries was, more or less, absent. That thirst for news from the distant scene of action, which became so distressing and lasted so long, had begun.

Mr. Henry Byng Harington, for many years the ornament of our bench, had just resigned his seat. His carriages were packed for a short journey to the hill station of Missouri. His route lay viâ Meerut; and from Missouri he was to have proceeded at once to Calcutta, to take his place as member (for the North-Western provinces) of the Legislative Council of India. His journey was stopped; and I may here remark that, with rare public spirit and self-devotion, he subsequently determined, at the desire of the Lieutenant-Governor, Mr. Colvin, to remain in Agra, though strongly tempted to place himself and his family in comparative security, by proceeding, as in the ordinary course of duty he was bound to do, to join his appointment in Calcutta.*

His advice was often most valuable to us all; and I only express the sentiments of the community of Agra, when recording our obligations to Mr. Harington for sharing our dangers and privations with us.

* The road *down* the country from Agra to Calcutta, viâ Mynpoorie and Cawnpore, was not closed to travellers for some days after the 11th May.

CHAP. II.

STATE OF THE COUNTRY BEFORE THE REVOLT.

BEFORE attempting to describe the immediate effect of the mutiny at Meerut and Delhi on the population of the North-Western provinces, I briefly sketch the state of things existing before the revolt.

The North-Western provinces, so called, are not now our most northern and western possessions in India, but obtained their designation before the Punjab was annexed. Stretching from the sources of the Ganges and Jumna on the north, to the Caramnasa on the south, the territory is parcelled out into six great divisions, comprising in all thirty-one zillahs or districts, with an area of 72,000 square miles, and a population of thirty millions.* Each division takes in five or six districts. At head-quarters (civil) in every division resides the Commissioner, with authority in police and revenue affairs over the district officers, designated "Magistrate and Collector" in each district of the division.

Courts of civil and criminal justice under Zillah Judges are held at the different stations, the juris-

* The reader who may wish for further statistical information is referred to Appendix A, in which the area, population, and revenue of the North-Western provinces are detailed.

diction of the judge extending over one, or sometimes two, districts.

The commissioners of revenue and police, the Zillah Judges, and the Collector Magistrate, all belong to the Covenanted Civil Service of the East India Company.

To superintend the working of this system, we had at Agra, when the mutiny broke out, a Lieutenant-Governor, the Sudder Court (Sudder Dewannie and Nizamut Adawlut*), and the Revenue Board.

Just one year before the mutiny, I was summoned from the Punjab to take my seat as a judge of the Sudder Court. Having been for three years Commissioner of Lahore, I had opportunities of comparing the systems of government in the Punjab and North-Western provinces. My prepossession in coming to Agra was in favour of the Punjab plan. I still retain that prepossession. I therefore, in describing the state of the North-Western provinces from May 1856, to May 1857, write without any prejudice in favour of the system of government within that territory, to which system, as will hereafter be shown, I entertain strong objections. But I had, as forming a part of the local administration,

* Chief civil and criminal tribunal. Has power of life and death. The judges formerly were the Governor-General and members of council; and now, under Her Majesty's warrant, have precedence in India over other civil officers not governors or members of the Executive or Legislative Councils. Appeals in civil cases of 1000*l.* and upwards, lie to Her Majesty in Council. In other cases the orders of the court are final.

excellent opportunities of observing the general working of the government and state of the people.

I have already described * the condition of the people in the North-Western provinces at the period of the annexation of the Punjab. Making some little abatement for the youth and zeal of the writer, I still adhere to that description, and on my return to the provinces from Lahore, I found no deterioration in the state of the people. Mr. Colvin, who in 1853 had succeeded Mr. Thomason as Lieutenant-Governor, had worked hard and well; the operations of the police were closely supervised, the Lieutenant-Governor watching the conduct of each Magistrate, I may almost say of every criminal case, with untiring vigilance; numerous proclaimed offenders, who had been at large for the last twenty years, had been apprehended and brought to trial. Murderous affrays were gradually becoming more rare.

It was no fault of Mr. Colvin's that our civil courts were still nearly as unpopular as ever. He had done what he could to reform them, and the tendency of legislation towards simplicity and ra-

* "Notes on the North-Western Provinces of India," published by Chapman and Hall in 1852. In alluding to this book, I would apologise by observing, that most of it was written when I was very young, and consequently in too ambitious a style. Since I wrote it, my feelings towards the people of India may have been changed by late events; but, nevertheless, the principles advocated in the Notes are, I believe, sound. It may be difficult hereafter to love the people of India, but we must nevertheless still cultivate their affections if we would hold the country.

pidity of procedure had been sufficiently marked. A great change* for the better was in contemplation, when the mutiny put a stop to all further progress in the road to civilisation.

In revenue matters I found the Collectors of districts more pressed than ever by the requirements of the government for information, statistics, &c., the fault of the system being, that too much detail of work done was expected. The pressure of the land revenue, as in former years, was generally equal; if not moderate, certainly not excessive. It was a full, but just land tax, firmly enforced, without any frequent resort to measures of distress, and on the whole punctually paid.

So far as the happiness of a nation consists in general peace, order, personal safety and liberty, with abundance of the necessaries of life, the people of the North-Western provinces were happy.

They disliked, for very sufficient reason, our system of civil procedure. The police, chosen from amongst themselves, and superintended by native subordinate magistrates, were unpopular, because every Asiatic man with power in his hands is apt to abuse that power, and at best to think too much of himself and too little of the public. Lastly, our village educational measures were disliked and suspected.

But, for all this, I repeat that the mass of the

* The new Code of Civil Procedure, prepared by Her Majesty's Commissioners in London, was about to be introduced when the mutiny broke out.

people were quiet and as contented as any semi-barbarous people can be with a strong government. Not a whisper of treason, rebellion, or disaffection was heard; agriculture and commerce were thriving, population increasing, when on this busy working scene broke the revolt.

CHAP. III.

AGRA IN THE MONTH OF MAY, 1857.

CIRCUMSTANCES prevented me from keeping up my accustomed regular journal, but I shall present to the reader occasional extracts from the short notes recorded, which will enable me to carry on the gloomy narrative of the past year, all reference to my own private sufferings being omitted.

"*Sunday, May* 10*th.* — A quiet day.

"*Monday,* 11*th.* — This Mofussilite Extra* was put into my hands. Harington was to have started for the hills this afternoon; he will pause.

"*Tuesday,* 12*th.* — Bishop Persico (Roman Catholic Bishop of Agra) and one of the French missionaries proceeding to Thibet, spent the evening with us. No regular post in from Allygurh this morning. The Meerut mails stopped by the mutineers.

"*Wednesday,* 13*th.*—Summoned to government house to take part in a council of war."

Here I pause to look back to that scene. Mr. Colvin had received reports from which he was led to suppose, that the mutineers from Meerut, after sacking Delhi and committing atrocities there, were marching on Agra. I found the Lieutenant-

* See ante, pages 1 to 2.

Governor already exposed to that rush of alarm, advice, suggestion, expostulation and threat, which went on increasing for nearly two months until he was driven broken-hearted into the fort. The critic may ask, why did Mr. Colvin allow any man to advise, threaten, or expostulate? My answer is, that his position from the first was one of extreme difficulty; he did his duty to the best of his ability, and his devotion to the public good ended only with his life. To say that he made some mistakes is to say that he was a man.

I was surprised to find that the Lieutenant-Governor had already taken into his confidence some of the Mahomedan high officials. Whilst talking, he handed me with a smile, one of the notes pouring in. It was from an able public officer, who had great opportunities of knowing what was going on in the city, and contained a solemn warning to His Honour to beware of the knife of the assassin.

One officer rushed in to suggest that we should all retire to the fort, another to ask what was to be done at the jail, a third to speak about provisions, a fourth about the sepoy regiments in cantonments. Every man was anxious to do his best, but to do it in his own way. It was decided to brigade the troops early next morning in the park surrounding Government House, the Brigadier to command, and the Lieutenant-Governor on his elephant to accompany the brigade, and so we were all to march out to meet the enemy.

After satisfying myself that at least a company

of the European regiment had been ordered into the fort, professedly to support, but in reality to over-awe the sepoys who had hitherto formed the garrison, and after expressing my doubt as to the fact of any mutineers being near us, I retired with Mr. Harington, promising to attend the Lieutenant-Governor in the morning.

"Mr. Thornhill, Secretary to Government, came with his family to our house to sleep, or rather to pass the night, for too many reports and notes came in to allow him much rest. He observed to me, that the sepoys held our forts, treasuries, and arsenals all over the country, and that if they rose at once upon us there was no European force to put them down. Matters certainly looked bad; however, the report of the advance of the mutineers upon Agra was contradicted.

"*Thursday*, 14*th*.—The troops were brigaded this morning, not at Government House, but at cantonments. The salute fired when Mr. Colvin came on parade frightened the ladies in the civil lines, as they supposed a fight between the Europeans and natives had begun. Colvin addressed the 3rd Europeans first, telling them to feel no distrust of their native fellow-soldiers, whom they should consider brothers in arms—(our honest fellows looked as if they would nevertheless like to have a shot at their brothers). He added, the rascals at Delhi have killed a clergyman's daughter, and if you should have to meet them in the field you will not forget this.

"Then came the sepoys' turn. The Lieutenant-

Governor said, that he fully trusted them, asked them to come forward if they had any complaints to make, and offered to discharge on the spot any man who wished to leave his colours. Prompted by their officers to cheer, the sepoys set up a yell; they looked, however, with a devilish scowl at us all. I rode through the city home, turning back crowds of East Indians and others who were struggling down to the fort. Many who had taken refuge there last night came out. Meerut mail in.

"*Friday*, 15*th*.—A stupid panic last night again; we slept at the Candaharie Bagh.* I patrolled with Muir, Thornhill, Dashwood and Lowe. Better rumours from Delhi, but no dak in thence or from Meerut. Telegraphic communication with Calcutta stopped."

Here I must record the indignation with which on Thursday evening we learned that the mutineers at Meerut, after firing the station, murdering our countrymen, women and children, and breaking the jail, had been permitted to retire quietly on Delhi, taking their barbers, water-carriers, bag and baggage, just as if they had been going an ordinary march. I now know that Major Rosser, of H. M. 6th Carbineers, asked permission to follow them with cavalry and guns. If he had been allowed to do so, it is quite possible, and indeed probable, that

* A masonry house belonging to the Rajah of Bhurtpore, and occupied by my colleague, Mr. Morgan, who kindly allowed it to be used as a stronghold for the "Civil Lines."

the mutiny, for the present at least, might have been crushed.

"*Saturday*, 16*th.*—Gwalior Contingent (small detachments of all arms) coming in. Orders from Meerut to throw the European regiment into the fort over-ruled by Mr. Colvin, who has received full power and authority from Lord Canning to act during the crisis as may seem best. Finding that Mr. Colvin wished to raise some Irregulars at Mynpoorie, I volunteered, and got written orders* to proceed and raise a couple of hundred men. But as I was making preparations, it was represented to Mr. Colvin that the departure of a Sudder Judge from Agra just now would add to the general alarm of the natives in the city; so he sent Thornhill to ask me to stay, thanking me handsomely for the offer.

"*Monday*, 18*th.*—Cheering news from Etaweh, of the 9th Native Infantry cutting up some of the

* Mr. Raikes is deputed to raise 200 cavalry in the Mynpoorie, Etaweh, Furuckabad, and Etah districts.

Pay. 20 rupees per mensem, certain for two years. Not to be employed beyond the division.

Duty. To protect roads, towns, villages, and poor people from plunder. The officers of all districts with whom Mr. Raikes is in communication to be told that they need not be under the least apprehension, and should not think of moving their families or property, or making any change whatever in their daily habits. The insurgents will be promptly and effectively put down.

All civil officers will co-operate with Mr. Raikes in carrying out these orders, and the collectors will honour his drafts.

(*Signed*) T. R. Colvin.

May 16th, 1857.

run-away troopers. At court some alarming letters from ———, who professes to know of some great impending dangers. The Gwalior Contingent men ask if the flour supplied to their camp is from government stores. If so they will not touch it. This is not pleasant, they have got hold of the bone dust story.*

"*Tuesday*, 19*th*.—The news from all sides seems good. Our native allies rallying around us, the European troops hastening down from the hills upon Delhi, and we hear that many Englishmen and women have escaped alive from Delhi.

"*Thursday*, 21*st*.—Heard of the fall of Allygurh to the mutineers. An alarm in the city, and a general rush to the Candaharee Bagh. I rode down and brought some ammunition from the jail to the bagh, in which hundreds of the Christian population had hastily assembled. I then rode to French's school; found French there alone, the other missionary having gone to look after his wife."

I must pause here to record the impression made upon my mind by the calmness and coolness of Mr. French. Every Englishman was handling his sword or revolver. The road covered with carriages, people hastening right and left to the rendezvous at Candaharee Bagh. The city folk

* One of the many inventions circulated amongst the sepoys, in order to produce disaffection, was, that the Government had cows' bones made into powder, and mixed with the flour sold in the bazaars, in order to pollute their food, a bone being an abomination in the eyes of the Hindoo.

running as for their lives, and screaming that the mutineers from Allygurh were crossing the bridge. The "*bud-maashes*"* twisting their moustachios and putting on their worst looks. Outside the college all alarm, hurry and confusion. Within calmly sate the good missionary, hundreds of young natives at his feet, hanging on the lips which taught them the simple lessons of the Bible. And so it was throughout the revolt. Native functionaries, highly salaried, largely trusted, deserted and joined our enemies, but the students at the government, and still more, the missionary, schools kept steadily to their classes; and when others doubted or fled, they trusted implicitly to their teachers and openly espoused the Christian cause.

I may add my belief that, owing partly to this good disposition of the students, and partly to the zeal of the missionary, Mr. French's missionary college was about the last to close and the first to re-open of all our public institutions at Agra, during the period of the revolt.

"*Friday*, 22*nd*.—Plenty of alarmists. In the morning I was assured that the Principal Sudder Ameen (native judge) was circulating seditious reports. I traced out the story and found it to be without foundation. In the evening ——— came over in the greatest excitement, having heard of

* Budmaash means a man of bad livelihood. Our Indian cities unfortunately teem with such characters, ripe for mischief and longing for anarchy.

the fall of Mynpoorie; this turned out to be untrue. A fire at night.

"*Saturday*, 23*rd*. — We went to see Lady Outram, who had been compelled to fly, as for her life, from Allygurh. She was suffering much from her feet, having been obliged to walk without shoes part of the way from Allygurh. To-day's alarm was that the Mahratta horse (part of Scindia's body guard sent to attend upon the lieutenant-governor) were to be sent away. I was just going at Muir's suggestion to remonstrate against this move with Colvin, when it was countermanded.

"*Sunday*, 24*th*.—We had a quiet night, attended divine service. Captain Greathed called to ask for a body of volunteers to escort the Gwalior guns towards Allygurh. I was just out on this business when I heard that the expedition was countermanded. Hassan Ali Thanadar (police superintendent), of Seersagunge (in the Mynpoorie district), came in. He says that John Power is holding his own well at Mynpoorie; and that Rao Bowannie Singh has taken the government treasury into his fort. I gave him letters to several leading men to encourage them to rally round Power just now.

"*Monday*, 25*th*. — The Eed festival is over, and people seem happier: fires at night now and then.

"*Tuesday*, 26*th*, up to end of the week.—Much anxiety about Indian affairs. Regiments mutinying right and left."

As I copy this journal the reminiscences of the period come full upon me. I pause for a moment to recall the past, and to describe our condition thus far.

As yet, setting panics aside, Agra had been quiet. No blood, either of natives or Europeans, had been shed. Yet, from the 11th May to the end of the month, every day and every night had been full of anxiety. Hitherto we had been the lords of the nations, flattered, courted by the people, caressed by fortune, confident in our own strength. How soon might we, like our Christian brethren and sisters at Delhi, be wanderers, houseless, with a blood-thirsty enemy on our track, or what at first we dreaded as much, shut up, amidst famine and pestilence, in a fort.

Amidst the civilization of the nineteenth century, among libraries, printing presses, colleges, and cathedrals, we found ourselves on the verge of barbarism.

Delhi too, had all these types of a thriving European civilization a few days back; now what remained at Delhi of western art, but ruins soaked with Christian blood? The sepoys of the 44th and 67th Regiments of Native Infantry, whose comrades at Delhi were revelling amongst the fragments of our churches and palaces, longed to bring about a like ruin at Agra. Nightly fires and secret meetings told us their temper. How soon might we expect them to throw off the mask of subordination, and carry fire and sword into our dwellings? How long would the Gwalior Contingent army remain staunch, with its infantry, cavalry, and powerful siege artillery? Their temper too had been shown; how many days more would they fawn upon the officers whom they had already marked for destruction? The youthful Scindia, with his passion for arms, and the traditions of the past burning in his breast, what chance was there of his fidelity? Mutiny had already broken out at Allygurh, who could calculate on the troops at Mynpoorie, Furuckabad, and Etaweh? Our own local police, on whom muskets and ball ammunition had been lavished, and who already began to scowl upon the Christian, how far were they to be trusted?

Such were the questions which perplexed the mind of every man capable of comprehending the gravity of the crisis. They who had friends or relations in Oude, Cawnpore, or Rajpootana, were further tormented by daily reports of fresh outbreaks, murders, and mutinies.

The men who cared least for all this were those most in danger, our young officers in the native regiments. They rode, swam, and played at billiards with as much gaiety as though they had not nightly to sleep in the lines amongst a set of ruffians thirsting for their blood. My own position and that of my colleagues was not an enviable one. With superior opportunities of knowing the extent of the dangers which overhung not only our wives, sisters, and children, but our empire in India; we were obliged daily to take our seat on the bench, and listen to long arguments about debts and mortgages, which we suspected would soon be cleared off by the intervention of anarchy rather than law. We had to grant injunctions which nobody attended to, and to pass decrees which no man could execute. And specially irksome was this mockery to one like me, who had near and dear relations at a distant station exposed to the full fury of the mutiny. At the same time the Sudder Court had no executive power, and was helpless, or nearly so, either for good or evil.

Amidst all these various causes for anxiety, the most immediate to the Christian community of Agra, was the hourly expectation of a local sepoy revolt. It was therefore a positive relief to me when, on the night of the 30th June, Messrs. Muir and Farquhar called, and told me that there had been mutiny and murder at Muttra, and that Government had determined to disarm the native regiments at daybreak next morning.

CHAP. IV.

SIR HENRY LAWRENCE AND HIS OLD STAFF.

I HAVE said that the detachments from the native infantry regiments, stationed at Muttra, mutinied on the night of Saturday the 30th. On the same night, at the same hour, the sepoys in the distant capital of Lucknow rose to a similar work of conflagration, robbery, mutiny, and murder. On the afternoon of Saturday, by the last regular post that for nearly a twelvemonth left Lucknow, Sir Henry Lawrence despatched the following letter to me.

"Lucknow, May 30th.

"MY DEAR RAIKES,

"Kindly give me an occasional line until Delhi is taken. We are pretty jolly, but if the commander-in-chief delay much longer he may have to recover Cawnpore, Lucknow, and Allahabad; indeed all down to Calcutta.

"We are in a funny position. While we are intrenching two posts in the city, we are virtually besieging four regiments (in a quiet way) with three hundred Europeans. Not very pleasant diversion to my civil duties. I am daily in the town four miles off for some hours, but reside in cantonments guarded by the gentlemen we are besieging!

"Send a copy of this to my brother George at Ajmere; my health is very good *for me*.

"Christian* is doing very well and pluckily.

* Sir Henry here alluded to my son-in-law, George Jackson Christian, Commissioner of Seetapore in Oude, who, with his wife and one child, perished on the 3rd June, in the massacre at that station. The remaining child, a little girl of three years, was rescued at the time by the heroism of Capt. Burnes, son of James and nephew of Sir Alexander and Charles, who, at the risk and, as events turned out, probably at the sacrifice of his own life, carried her off in his arms. She shared the captivity of this noble-hearted man with Miss Jackson and Mrs. Orr, and sunk under her sufferings, in Lucknow, after several months' imprisonment.

Her preserver was put to death, at an earlier period, by the sepoys, thus adding to the list of martyrs which the brave family of Burnes has produced.

On the very day, May 30th, when Sir Henry thus briefly eulogised my son-in-law, George Christian too was writing to me his last letter, in which he thus alluded to the state of affairs.

. . . .

"All quiet here; and, throughout my division, the people seem well disposed, and the regular regiment here, the 41st, are quite quiet.

"And I have in position 950 men, so that, if things go wrong elsewhere, and they are tempted to rise, we could (D.F.) crush them in an hour.

"Our position here is strong, and our force so *mixed* (an important point now-a-days), that I am prepared to send, if required, reinforcements to the tune of 250 soldiers of the 9th Oude Irregular Infantry in any direction, and still retain enough to thrash the 41st Native Infantry.

"Throughout the province there is quiet, and at every station preparations have been made. . . . .

What I most fear are risings in the districts and the Irregulars getting tainted. Daily I have reports of conspiracies all around. Show this to Mr. Colvin and Reid.*

"Yours very sincerely,
"H. LAWRENCE."

Every Englishman will forgive me if I wander from my subject for a moment, to offer my humble tribute of affection to the man who, perhaps above all others, has done honour to the name of English-

"Sir Henry Lawrence has arranged admirably, and come what will, we are prepared. . . . . . .

"The village system, which makes all men equal in their poverty, is now fairly on its trial in the disturbed districts, and government has hardly a single man of influence to look to in them. Their army is the same, a dead level; no gentlemen, no difference save in military rank.

"I love neither system, but I hope our eyes will now be opened to Robertson's prophecy on the inevitable tendency of our system."

I have been told by native fugitives from Seetapore, that when the 41st mutinied George Christian called out his Irregulars, who gradually deserted as the sepoys approached. Although my son-in-law treated the matter so lightly in this his last letter, I knew from former letters and from other sources that he had been warned, not only of the prevailing disaffection in Oude, but also that, either owing to his name or character, he had long been marked by the 41st regiment as the first Englishman to be shot at Seetapore. Capt. Orr had, to my knowledge, written to warn him. However, as Sir Henry writes, George Christian was, like his brethren in both services, doing "pluckily," and, like too many of them, he and all that belonged to him perished.

* Reid means E. A. Reade, an old friend of Sir Henry, member of the Revenue Board at Agra.

man in India. To know Sir Henry was to love him.

In 1853, when I was on my way to Lahore, and Sir Henry was leaving the Punjab, I had witnessed the unbounded regard which all classes displayed to his person. During my term of office at Lahore, I had occasion, in the discharge of my public duty, to prosecute and bring to punishment men who owed their appointments to Sir Henry's favour. Instead of resentment, he honoured me with increased regard, acknowledging that I had exercised a necessary severity. In March, 1857, at Agra, when on his way to take charge of his new duties as Chief Commissioner of Oude, I had much daily and unreserved intercourse with Sir Henry. I found him, as it were, ripening fast, alike for that goal of human glory which he was soon to attain, and for that sublimer change which so quickly awaited him.

His heart seemed overflowing with Christian charity. I remember that, in returning a volume of Memoirs of Bishop Sandford, he wrote to call my attention to the following passage, which he had marked with a pencil. "My fears for those who retain a spirit of unforgiveness are overpowering: I will sincerely declare to you, that I could not myself pray to God or ask His pardon for my many transgressions before I go to bed at night with any comfort, or with any hope of being heard, unless I were conscious that I did from my heart forgive as I ask to be forgiven." (Vol. ii. pp. 106, 107.) When next I met him, as we walked to the early church service (it was the time of Lent), he poured out his heart on the beautiful topic of Christian forgiveness, adding, that he had sent a copy of the extract above quoted to a distinguished officer, once his friend, who had taken deep offence at some public act of Sir Henry's. For every child that he met in my own family, in the missionary or other public schools, he had a word of kindness or encouragement. Incidentally he told me that the secret of his ability to support those public institutions with which his name will for ever be associated, was to be found in his abstinence to the utmost from all sorts of personal expense. During his stay in Agra, while his hand was open to every one else, he resolutely avoided spending money on himself.

He went to Oude, not without feelings of ambition, but principally from a high sense of duty, whilst he had the strongest medical opinions of the necessity of an immediate change to Europe, and when suffering, as he told me, "from a dozen different complaints."

At that moment I was preparing a little publication on the Punjab. Sir Henry asked me to visit him at Lucknow in the following September, when he would place all his private papers* connected with his Punjab career at my disposal.

With this same object in view I applied to Colonel Herbert Edwardes, on his journey viâ

* Sir Henry's papers had been sent to Bombay, at which port he had proposed to embark when he was stopped by Lord Canning's summons to Lucknow.

Agra to Peshawur, on his return from Lucknow in April, 1857, to give me a memorandum of Sir Henry's old staff in the Punjab previous to annexation.

Colonel Edwardes, as ready with his pen as with his sword, as all the world knows, very kindly noted down for me the following graphic description. The public will thank me for throwing open this little gallery of portraits. One of the originals, John Nicholson, has, alas! gone down already to the hero's grave amidst the tears of his countrymen, under the walls of Delhi.

Sir Henry's "Old Staff" in the Punjab previous to annexation.

ARTHUR COCKS.	EDWARD LAKE.
GEORGE LAWRENCE.	JOHN R. BECHER.
JAMES ABBOTT.	JOHN NICHOLSON.
GEORGE M'GREGOR.	HERBERT EDWARDES.
HARRY LUMSDEN.	REYNELL TAYLER.

ARTHUR COCKS

was the "chief assistant to the resident" when Sir Henry Lawrence was administering the Punjab for the Maharajah. He imbibed all Sir Henry's feelings, and became greatly attached to the chiefs and people. He hardly stayed a year after annexation, and left the Punjab because he could not bear to see the fallen state of the old officials and sirdars. (He had been unfortunately made Deputy Commissioner of Lahore, where he saw this *only:* had he got a country district he would have been happy, I believe, in the real good of the lower orders.) He has carried Sir Henry's feelings with him to the North Western Provinces, and acknowledges him as "the good genius" of his public *creed*. The Sudder Court of Agra can best judge if the creed be orthodox.*

GEORGE LAWRENCE

was Sir Henry's elder brother, and formed his own character. Best as a soldier. Held command of Peshawur during the second Sikh war of 1848-49, and kept the large Sikh garrison from overt rebellion up to a very late period of the war.

Left the Punjab when it became a purely civil administration.

Is now officiating agent to the Governor-General in Rajpootana.

JAMES ABBOTT,

when assistant-resident, was deputed by Sir Henry to receive charge of the Huzara frontier from Maharajah Goolab Singh (to whom it had been originally assigned, but who proved utterly unable to control it; thus leading to an exchange of

* In reply to this allusion, I can only say that the Sudder Court hold Mr. Arthur Cocks in the very highest esteem; my own opinion of his noble character and conduct will be given further on.

territory—Huzara reverting to the Sikhs and they giving up some quiet tracts to the Squeezer!)

James Abbott was instructed to reduce the revenue of Huzara to something nominal as the only way of re-peopling and pacifying the country. He did so; going from valley to valley with his mission of hope; and won the confidence of the tribes.

He remained among them afterwards as coadjutor of the Sikh governor, Sirdar Chuttur Singh, the father-in-law of Maharajah Duleep Singh. In 1848, the Sirdar headed the Sikh insurrection, and James Abbott found himself placed, like others of Sir Henry's assistants, in the strange position of raising the Mahomedan subjects of the Sikhs against the rebel Sikh chiefs, to preserve if possible the Sikh raj, of which the British government was guardian.

The mountaineers of Huzara could not contend with the Sikh brigades, but they remained faithful to James Abbott, and protected him for many months, till the battle of Goojarat ended the campaign. Then followed annexation and the introduction of a system of civil administration throughout the Punjab. James Abbott became Deputy Commissioner of Huzara, and remained so till 1853, when he resigned the charge. Thus he was six years in Huzara; and he left it amidst the unfeigned regrets of the people. During his rule, exiles driven out by the Sikhs ten, twenty, thirty, forty years before, had flocked back again from beyond the border, and been resettled on their paternal lands;—Huzara had passed from a desolation to a smiling prosperity;—it was *he* who had worked the change—a single Englishman;—he had literally lived among them as their patriarch—an out-of-door, under-tree life; every man, woman and child in the country knew him personally, and hastened from their occupations to welcome and salute him as he came their way.

The children especially were his favourites. They used to go to "Kâkâ Abbott" (Uncle Abbott) whenever their mouths watered for fruit or sugar-plums. He never moved out without sweetmeats in his pocket for the chance children who might meet him, and as plentiful a supply of money for the poor. He literally spent all his substance on the people, and left Huzara, it is believed, with only his month's pay.

His last act was to invite the country—not the neighbours—but all Huzara, to a farewell feast on the Nârâ hill; and there for three days and nights he might be seen with long grey beard over his breast, and grey locks far down his shoulders, walking about among the groups of guests, and hecatombs of pots and cauldrons—the kind and courteous host of a whole people.

What is the result?

The district of Huzara, which was notorious for its long continued struggles with the Sikhs, is now about the quietest, happiest, and most loyal in the Punjab.

JOHN BECHER

is James Abbott's successor; and is to Huzara all that Abbott *was*. High praise. His cutcherry is not "from ten till four" by the regulation clock; but all day, and at any hour of the night that anybody chooses; — the "*barahduree*" system of administration—living in a house with twelve doors, and all open to the people.

He was at Buttala before—and did the same there.*

GEORGE MACGREGOR,

now resident at Moorshedabad, was another of Sir Henry's assistants; but he had achieved his own

* I had the happiness of being associated with John Becher, who served under me as deputy commissioner of Buttala when I was commissioner of Lahore. When he left Buttala for Huzara, the people followed him in crowds, weeping and invoking blessings on his head. As a sample of "the school of Henry Lawrence," I give an extract from a kind letter which I received from Major Becher on my departure from Lahore for Agra.

. . . .

"Let me also on paper shake you by the hand, and wish 'Good bye' to you and to Mrs. Raikes in the same spirit as the 'Good-bye' at Umritsur, when I first met you, and all were giving an affectionate farewell to their old friend and master, Sir Henry Lawrence.

"Some day I may meet you again, and recall old memories of the Punjab, though I am sure you will never forget the Punjab portion of your life, nor will the Punjab be forgetful of you.

"May much of its *old spirit* remain!

"Huzara, March 28, 1856."

fame, and formed his own style, as political officer to the garrison of Jellalabad.

Major Harry Lumsden,

of the Guides, was picked out from his corps by Sir Henry Lawrence, and has proved the prince of border soldiers. He raised the Guide Corps; armed it with rifles; dressed it in mud-colour; and in endless skirmishes achieved a name with it which is as well known in Affghanistan as India. It has since been the model for the Punjab Irregular Force. He has now been selected to watch the Persians at Candahar—a high mark of the confidence of government.

Edward Lake

is another of Sir Henry's assistants;—but he was detached under Sir John Lawrence in the Jalundhur Doab, and must rather be regarded as a disciple of both brothers, uniting the best points of both systems. Brave—kind—active—indefatigable—accessible—thoughtful—chivalrous and wise:—he was as much at home as a soldier leading on the Bhawulpoor army at Mooltân—as he is in administering a highly organised system of civil government. As a leader he lived among his soldiers; as a civilian he lived among the people. By both he has been loved and respected. He may be taken as the best type the Punjab affords of the military civilian.

Of what class is

JOHN NICHOLSON

the type then? Of none, for truly he stands alone. But he belongs essentially to the school of Henry Lawrence.

I only knocked down the walls of the Bunnoo *forts*.

John Nicholson has since reduced the *people* (the most ignorant, depraved and blood-thirsty in the Punjab) to such a state of good order and respect for the laws, that in the last year of his charge not only was there no murder, burglary, or highway robbery, but not an *attempt* at any of those crimes.

The Bunnoochees, reflecting on their own metamorphosis in the village gatherings under the vines, by the streams they once delighted so to fight for, have come to the conclusion that "the good Mahomedans" of historic ages must have been "just like Nikkul Seyn!" They emphatically approve him as every inch a hâkim. And so he is. It is difficult to describe him. He must be seen. Lord Dalhousie,—no mean judge—perhaps best summed up his high military and administrative qualities, when he called him "a tower of strength." I can only say that I think him equally fit to be Commissioner of a division, or General of an army. Of the strength of his personal character, I will only tell two anecdotes.

1. If you visit either the battle field of Goojarat, or Cheyleanwallah—the country people begin

their narrative of the battles thus, " Nikkul Seyn stood just *there!*"

2. A brotherhood of Fakeers in Huzara abandoned all forms of Asiatic monachism, and commenced the worship of Nikkul Seyn ;—which they still continue! Repeatedly they have met John Nicholson since, and fallen at his feet as their Gooroo.* He has flogged them soundly on every occasion, and sometimes imprisoned them; but the sect of the Nikkul Seynees remains as devoted as ever. " Sanguis martyrorum est semen Ecclesiæ."

On the last whipping John Nicholson released them, on the condition that they would transfer their adoration to John Becher;—but arrived at their monastery in Huzara, they once more resumed the worship of the relentless Nikkul Seyn.

REYNELL TAYLER

was another of the old set, and the whole set is proud of him. He set siege to the border fort of Lukkee, in the war of 1848—49, with a handful of Mooltânee soldiers, sapped his way regularly up to the walls, and reduced the garrison to surrender. He held charge of Bunnoo for two years after annexation, and has published the best account of that district. His character is so *round* and perfect in its goodness, that one is almost as provoked with him, as the Athenians with Aristides.

He got a right manly slash down his face, in charging the Sikh cavalry at Moodkee, or his gentleness and goodness would be worthy of a woman.

* Religious or spiritual guide.

Such were the instruments used by Sir Henry Lawrence. How much England owes him at this moment who shall say? I will try to recount what the early Punjab Administration has to thank him for, and here again I am greatly assisted by the kindness of Colonel Edwardes.

First.—The men he had about him; and the high standard of public duty, zeal, personal exertion, and love of the people of the country with which he inspired them. These were the nucleus of the new Administration.

Secondly.—The personal confidence of all classes in a Government over which Sir Henry presided, It was soon known to the Sikhs and chiefs of all kinds that the Governor-General was determined to reduce the Punjab into a British Province, and that John Lawrence, with the aid of George Christian the Secretary to the Board of Administration, would push on vigorously the great change.—Sir Henry interposed with equal vigour, and worked for a transition instead of a revolution.—He eased off every falling interest with the tender compassion of a friend who had known the class in better days. He got a little more for every one. He fought every losing battle for the old chiefs and jaghire dars with entire disregard for his own interest, and at last left the Punjab, to use Colonel Edwardes' words, "dented all over with defeats and disapprovals, honourable scars in the eyes of the bystanders."

Thirdly.—Colonel Edwardes believed that Sir Henry was the proposer of the disarming of the people of the Punjab. Whoever originated this important step, I know Sir Henry cordially enforced and approved of it.

Fourthly.—He raised the Punjab Irregular Force. Lord Dalhousie gave him *all* the appointments. This is the force which took so leading a part in the siege of Delhi, and without which it is not too much to say that we could hardly have effected the reduction of that mutinous stronghold.

Fifthly.—He originated jail reform in the Punjab, abolished the "night chain" and other abominations, introduced in-door labour, and placed all the prisons of the province under one Inspector. His *personal* labours in this matter, going from jail to jail, rooting out abuses, rising even at midnight to visit the prisoners' barracks, thus inspiring his civil subordinates with the idea of "kindness to the captive"; all this evinced the strength and reality of his feelings of humanity. Sir Henry was pre-eminently the friend of *the man who is down;* thieves and convicts not excepted. In all and every good work of this nature he was ably supported by Mr. Montgomery, but Sir Henry had long been at this labour of love before Montgomery came to the Punjab as Commissioner of Lahore.

Lastly (I will not dilute the following note of Colonel Edwardes by a word of my own).

"What distinguished the Punjab Administration in India, was *the simplicity of the Courts of Justice*, their cheapness, accessibility, and promptness; the exclusion of Vakeels; the confronting of the real parties; the arbitration by Punchâyuts.

"I believe that this was *very largely* due to Sir Henry. He was not intimately acquainted with the organisation of the Courts of the North Western Provinces, but in his duties of Revenue Surveyor, had gathered the impression, in village talks, &c. &c., that those Courts were hard of approach, technical in operation, and expensive even in their happiest issues! It fell in, therefore, with all his instincts to avoid these results in the Punjab machinery; and when the Code was being drawn up his vote was strong for simplicity, and expedition, and publicity. In this matter he was certainly *not alone*, for John knew the weaknesses of the system in which he had been raised *still better* than Henry, and was resolved to have a much simpler procedure. I am under the idea that we owe it to John that the revenue, civil and criminal functions, were united in the district officers, which is practically the key-stone of our arch. That came of John knowing the details, and seeing his way to the remedy. The Code in fact was drawn up by John, and owes its working efficiency to him. But what I mean is, that Sir Henry was ever at John's elbow, calling out for the great principles of cheap justice.

"Besides this, he was for ever talking the new officers into his own views; and influencing them to live among the people, to do as many cases under trees, and as few under the punkah, as possible; to ride about their districts and see and hear for themselves, instead of through the police and

Omlah, and his cheery earnest way of doing this, his glad praise of any rough and ready officer, and his indignant contempt for all skulks, idlers, and *nimmuk-hurâm*, drew *models* on young fellows' minds which they went forth and copied in their administrations — it sketched a *faith*, and begot a *school*, and they are both living things to this day. I have no hesitation in saying that he has exercised the greatest personal influence for good of all the men in the Punjab government."

It will not be supposed, from the above remarks, that I wish to disparage the labours and efforts of other men, and to eulogise the dead at the expense of the living. We owe it to Lord Dalhousie that three such men as the two Lawrences and Montgomery exercised so vast an influence over the twelve millions of the Punjab.

His Lordship placed at the Board of Administration, Henry Lawrence, as well as John Lawrence, and Robert Montgomery.

England, or rather Ireland, may well be proud of such sons as these. Five and thirty years back this remarkable trio were playfellows at a little school in the North of Ireland. Five years ago they formed the Board which ruled the destinies of the Punjab, and devised (with the aid of Mr. Mansel and under the valuable auspices of Lord Dalhousie) that scheme of government which must one day dominate over the Indian Peninsula.

Now, the one rules over the Punjab, having justly been hailed, within the last twelve months, the Saviour of Upper India.

The other, equally honoured and beloved by his countrymen, is stilling the troubled sea of insurrection in Oude.

The third, now alas, beyond the reach of human praise, lives only here in the hearts of his friends, and the gratitude of the English Nation.*

* Sir H. Lawrence was as well suited for the duty of *pacification* as was Sir John for the work of administration. Conciliation was the forte of one, governing was the instinct of the other. Therefore, when the work of conciliation was over, Lord Dalhousie showed a wise discretion (in my humble opinion) when he left the task of mere administration in the hands of Sir John Lawrence.

CHAP. V.

AGRA IN JUNE, 1857.

To return to Agra. On the 30th May, at midnight, Mr. Muir and Dr. Farquhar called at the Candaharee Bagh, to tell us that a company of the regiment of Native Infantry sent out to relieve the guard over the treasury at Muttra, had mutinied, shooting down their officer, and then pursuing the course — now a routine one — of firing the houses of the English and breaking the prisons.

Mr. Colvin, with the advice of Mr. Drummond, the Magistrate, had at length wisely determined to disarm our two regiments of Sepoys. It became necessary for us, in the event of any outbreak on the part of these men, some of whom were posted at the Central Jail, in the heart of the Civil Station, to protect ourselves and the many defenceless Christian men, women, and children around. My colleague, Mr. Morgan, kindly allowed his house to be made a rendezvous in case of danger. Notices were sent round, and early in the morning of Sunday, some hundreds of all ranks and ages had congregated at the Candaharee Bagh, the men armed with swords and revolvers, the women generally dragging children and ayahs. We fell naturally under the command of Colonel Fraser, Chief Engineer of the North-Western Provinces, a fine old officer who had won his decoration as C.B. by an act of heroism in Burmah during the last campaign. Musquets and ammunition were served out, a chain of sentries posted, and the house began to be transformed from an elegant garden pavilion into a rough uncouth-looking fortress. In the military lines, the native regiments were drawn up on parade, a battery of artillery, under Captain D'Oyley, and the 3rd Europeans under Colonel Riddell, in a position to enforce obedience. The word "pile arms" was given. There was a moment of hesitation, a look of discontent. The officers sternly reiterated the order. Silent and sullen, the Sepoys obeyed—piled their arms, and were marched off to the lines. The 44th and 67th Regiments, whose colours had waved from the Indus to the Brahmapootra, were no more.

On examining the musquets, many were found loaded with ball. It was afterwards well known, that on this very Sunday morning, the Sepoys had conspired to overpower the European regiment when in Church, to rush upon the guns, and then to shoot, plunder and burn from one end of Agra to the other.

Whilst this was passing, five miles away from us, in the cantonments, a less successful manœuvre was executed close at hand. A detachment of the 3rd Europeans was marched suddenly up in front of the company of Sepoys on guard at the jail. The men imagined that an attack was intended, and ran in all directions, carrying their arms, and threatening to shoot any one who came near them. My young friend, Lieutenant Williams, who had left our garrison at Candaharee Bagh to reconnoitre, met some of these men, who began loading their musquets, vociferating and abusing him. Placing his hand in his breast, he told them to fire; on this they slunk away abashed, and most of them eventually gave up their arms, on reaching cantonments.

We were all very glad at Candaharee when Mr. Thornhill, the Secretary to Government, who had been to the cantonments to see the Lieutenant-Governor's order carried out, told us that the regiments had surrendered their arms. I set to work at once, with Colonel Fraser's full consent, to organise a permanent guard for the Candaharee Bagh. Stout English clerks, sun-burnt old soldiers on the pension list, Roman Catholic artillerymen who had fought under Scindia, East Indian sectioners, record keepers and tradesmen,—such was my material. As the Candaharee Bagh was now officially recognised by the Government as one of the chief places of rendezvous in the event of an émeute, I was well supplied with beer and biscuit for the garrison. Hundreds of large water vessels were ranged around the outer verandahs, sand bags were piled. The twelve o'clock gun * was

* The distance of the Civil Lines from the Cantonments was so great, that we had a separate gun daily fired at 12 o'clock.

dragged from its wonted site, and placed in a position to command the entrance into the Bagh. Grape shot were extemporised at a neighbouring coachmaker's shop, and, in short, we prepared ourselves to hold out in case of a sudden attack either from Sepoys, town mobs, prisoners, or the revolted regiments from Nusseerabad, which we knew were marching upon Agra.

I also raised, and with the liberal assistance of the Government equipped, a troop of Horse Volunteers. These men were intended by me to act as mounted police and patrols, and in the event of what we all daily and nightly expected, a "rush to the Fort," were to protect and escort the women and children for three miles from the Civil Lines through the city to the Fort. I at first commanded them in person, Major Prendergast kindly consenting to act under my orders. Early in June, with the assistance of Lieutenant Hugo James, who was also attached to the troop, I proceeded to Futtehabad to bring in the ladies and children from Etaweh. Although some person, I know not who, was good enough to send an account of this little expedition to the papers at the time, when an unmerited amount of praise was given to a very ordinary performance, I think it right, in order to subserve my prominent object of describing faithfully the state of the country and people, to sketch the expedition.

A little before sunset on the evening of the 15th June, our little party, consisting of Mr. Phillipps, the Magistrate of Etah, Lieutenant Hugo James, and the troop of thirty or forty Horse Volunteers under my command, marched from the Candaharee Bagh, through the city of Agra, towards Futtehabad.* Passing the Catholic Church and Convent, we were loudly cheered by the inmates. I recollect nothing of the night march except the astonishing quantity of water which we drank at every well on the road-side. But for the streaming perspiration no human skin could have contained the amount of liquid poured into us. Yet, just at this burning period, our poor countrymen and women were being hunted like wild beasts, *day and night*, all over Upper India.

Before day-break we reached Futtehabad. The citizens were in a state of anxious alarm. The rough Goojurs and Jats from Scindia's side of the Chumbul, were pouring down upon our villages, plundering, burning, and murdering all who resisted. The Thanadar had been surprised by them in a neighbouring village, and with difficulty escaped. A town watch had been hastily organised by the local police. The Tehsildar (native chief of revenue and police) and Moonsiff (native judge) received us with delight into the Tehseel station, a large straggling native fort. Both were in a state of the highest excitement; they had been repeatedly threatened with a visit from the Trans-Chumbul dacoits; the town was to be looted and their heads stuck upon the walls.

* This town is about twenty-five miles from the Civil Lines in a south-easterly direction. It is situated between the Jumna and the Chumbul rivers.

Soon after our arrival, whilst I was trying to get a short sleep on the Tehsildar's charpoy, an alarm was given. Lights were seen in the distance, there was a sound of men, horses, and carriages. The Tehsildar, putting a cap on his gun, declared that at last the enemy was upon us. It turned out, as I hoped and expected, that the cavalcade approaching consisted of the ladies and children from Etaweh, escorted by a detachment of Sepoys of the Gwalior Contingent, Irregular Cavalry, and some loyal Rajah's match-lock men, under the command of a very spirited and intelligent young Englishman, Mr. W. H. Parker.

As our presence afforded merely a temporary protection to the Tehsildar, I wrote at his request to Luchmun Singh, the chief of the Goojurs, and to another talook-dar in the immediate neighbourhood, for a couple of hundred match-lock men and some horse to assist in maintaining the authority of Government in Futtehabad. Under ordinary circumstances an order of this sort would have been promptly attended to; it was an unpleasant sign of the times that this answer came—"Luchmun Singh was much afraid that his men would join the marauders in their meditated attack on the town and Tehseel station." The fact was, these men had heard of the revolt of the Gwalior Contingent, and considered that the days of the British rule were numbered, and that in self-defence it was necessary for them to keep on good terms with Scindia's subjects.

The jemadar of the guard of Sepoys very sulkily counted over the ladies, children, and nurses, to me, and from his surly conduct I conclude that he had already heard how his brethren in arms at Gwalior had been rioting in the blood of our countrymen. It was a great happiness to have the party safe, and to conduct them without any alarm to Agra, on the night of June 16th. On reaching the Candaharee Bagh, we heard first that the Gwalior Contingent had mutinied, secondly that Delhi had fallen to our arms. The first report was unhappily too true; the last, to our sorrow, proved false.

As our fate at Agra depended much on the conduct of Scindia and his Contingent force, I turn to notice their conduct.

Gwalior is about seventy miles south-west of Agra, on the great road to Bombay. The Contingent force, of which the greater part was posted at Gwalior, consisted of five companies of artillery, with a magazine and siege train (3rd class), two cavalry and seven infantry regiments, under the command of Brigadier Ramsay. When the mutiny at Meerut broke out, the Lieutenant-Governor at once applied at Gwalior for cavalry and artillery. There was nothing in the conduct of the men who came to Agra to make us suppose that they would separate themselves from the Sepoys in general; nay, they rather piqued themselves on belonging to the army, and, as is usual with Contingent forces, looked up with respect to the regulars. If then the Bengal army was turning against us, we had no reason to hope that the

Gwalior Contingent would continue on our side. True, their officers, with that over-weening yet manly confidence to which nothing but a bullet could put a period, believed in their men. Nobody else did; certainly not Major Macpherson, Political Agent at the court of Scindia. His eyes were soon opened. The Maharaja told him plainly enough that the soldiers of the Contingent would soon follow the example of Meerut and Delhi. In nightly conference it was determined to rise, burn, and slay. Women and children alone were to be spared. In the meantime, until the fitting day arrived, the British officers were to be cajoled. And so it was. There was no reserve on the awful subject of the mutiny. Officers freely talked to their men; and their native subordinates, who in the lines were settling the propitious day and hour for cutting the throats of every Englishman, boasted, with tears in their eyes, how they would revenge the murders of Delhi and Meerut; and cursed the villains whose example they had determined to follow. Our officers would not allow themselves to suspect the men who had served them so long and so well. Meerut, Delhi, Allyghur, Muttra, had fallen, all around was falling; yet they refused to believe that their men, though of the same stock and stuff, could fail. They were ready to seal their faith, not only with their blood, but with what they prized far dearer, the blood of their wives and children. These true-hearted, faithful English gentlemen could not discern the mainspring of the machinery which was at work around them. What the Sepoys wanted was, to transfer their allegiance from England to the Mogul or to Scindia, or whoever might employ them, at once, as a body, complete and in perfect organisation. A rabble was to be picked up in every suburb; but an army, in a full state of discipline and equipment—this was a prize for which any monarch might bid high. It was, therefore, the policy of the native officers not only to conceal their treachery, but also to maintain to the last moment every sign and mark of the most perfect subordination and discipline.

We at Agra watched Gwalior anxiously. I had particular reasons for disquiet. Not only my friends, Major Macpherson and his sister, Mrs. Innes, were there in danger, but my kinsman, Major Raikes, had taken a part of his regiment, the 1st Gwalior Cavalry, to Mynpoorie, leaving his wife and infant with Major and Mrs. Blake, at Gwalior.

It had been decided by the military authorities that the ladies should not be removed, as the Sepoys were considered worthy of trust. So when the mutiny broke out, these delicate creatures were exposed to the fury of the revolt. On my return to Agra from Futtehabad, on hearing that the Political Agent, Major Macpherson, and several other refugees, had arrived from Gwalior, I wrote to him, enclosing a letter to my cousin, from my wife. I received the following reply from Mrs. Innes, the sister of Major Macpherson. It will serve to depict the scenes passing near us at this moment.

"I opened your note, as my brother is asleep, not ill, but much exhausted by exposure on the journey and anxiety.

"I deeply grieve that I must return Mrs. Raikes' note. We have some hope there may yet be good news of her, but we have reason to fear the worst. It is not certainty. Mrs. Raikes may have escaped, but Major Blake, in whose house she was, we know was mortally wounded at the beginning; and of Mrs. Blake and Mrs. Raikes we have been able to hear nothing. It is so utterly heart-breaking that I cannot venture to let myself realise it yet. We and many others have been mercifully preserved, but there are no fewer than eight ladies still unaccounted for, and that at least four or five of these were shot we have too little reason to doubt. However, some of them may have been defended and hidden. I had just written a note to Mrs. Raikes, but think it better to send this to you. It is so miserable a story that either to think or write of it is at present too much.

"Will you tell Mrs. Raikes that I should be very grateful to her for any change of dress she could afford me? Any sort of old thing until I can make other arrangements. I scarcely know what I have written, but only require an hour's sleep to make me all right.

"I hope you and Mrs. Raikes are as well as you can be in such sad and trying times, &c."

On the next day we had the happiness of receiving our cousin. Like hundreds of our country-women, she had been driven rudely from her home, exposed to the fury of an Indian sun and to the jests of the Sepoy rabble. Happier than many, her husband as yet was safe, and her child, and her courage had never failed for a moment.

She described her adventures thus:—On the afternoon of Sunday, 13th June, a building near the Mess House had been burnt; the Sepoys rushing to put out the flames, the usual trick to avert suspicion. Some, however, were overheard to say, we shall have a finer blaze to-night. Late in the evening, as Mrs. Blake and Mrs. Raikes were going to bed, shots were fired, flames began to ascend on all sides. The critical moment had come. The Contingent was in mutiny. Guards were posted by the mutineers on the roads to shoot down every officer who attempted to pass. Major Blake, a man who had devoted his whole life to his men, galloping towards the lines was shot down by the soldiers of another regiment. His own men, strange to say, wept as they watched his life-blood oozing away, and called loudly for medical aid when all aid was too late. When Major Blake rode off, his servants, seeing a body of mutineers coming down to the house, hastily concealed the ladies, child, and native wet nurse in a stable. The Reverend Mr. Coopland* and his wife afterwards joined them. Subsequently they were obliged to take shelter in a small outhouse. The Sepoy wretches, too cowardly to come in at the

* Military Chaplain at Gwalior.

door, got upon the roof and fired down. All were driven out. The Sepoys spared the women but seized the clergyman. He said, "I am not a fighting man, but a padre." * So much the worse, was their reply. He was shot down. Some men of the infantry, after the ladies had been deprived of their rings, escorted them to Scindia's Palace, which is some miles from the Cantonment. All the ladies, except Mrs. Stewart, were saved. She with her husband was murdered, I believe by the artillerymen.

Sometimes in covered carts, sometimes walking, these delicate creatures, with little but their sleeping dresses on them, without covering on their heads, had reached Agra.

The following letter, addressed about this time to me, by Captain D'Oyly, will be read with great interest by all who remember how nobly, all mangled and bleeding from his death wound, he fought his battery on the memorable 5th of July.

"I have just seen Campbell, and have had a long chat with him regarding the two artillery ladies, who, with their families, are still supposed to be at or near Gwalior.

"It would appear, that when Campbell yesterday morning was pushing on towards Gwalior, to meet his wife, &c., he fell in with a Sowar of the 1st Regiment Gwalior Irregulars (Alexander's). This man told him that he had heard from another native, that both Mrs. Hawkins and Mrs. Stewart, with

* The word commonly used all over India for a minister of religion.

their children, were safe, and were under the protection of the Maharaja. Campbell says that he has no reason whatever to doubt this man's story.

"He is of opinion that no attempt had better be made by Europeans to assist in rescuing, protecting, or escorting these two ladies, that, most likely if the people under whose charge they now are, heard that a party of 'Gora-log' (Europeans) were coming down to rescue the ladies, they might get exasperated, and destroy the persons whom they are now protecting; under these circumstances, I think we have no alternative but to follow Campbell's advice.

"I fear, therefore, we must leave them to their fate, hoping for the best, and should any tidings be received to the effect that these ladies had left the places where they now may be, and were attempting to get into Agra, then the services of a party of your Horse might be of great use."

The following note also is characteristic of the spirit of my gallant young friend, Lieutenant Hugo James.

"Many thanks for allowing me to peruse D'Oyly's letter; perhaps Campbell's advice is the best.

"However, I shall always be ready to move out at a moment's notice, should it be necessary."

As the sad month of June passed on, the Government determined to raise militia, horse and foot, and place the levies under military law and military leaders. Mr. Harington came to me and said that it was considered in the cantonments that it would be conducive to the public good, if I would resign the command of my Horse to Major Prendergast, to be employed in the cantonments. Suffering as I was from low fever, and distracted by private calamity, I was obliged to confess that I had no qualities left in me to compensate for my ignorance of military tactics. I accordingly drew up a short address to my men, thanking them for their services, and informing them that it had been intimated to me that the formation of one strong corps of mounted militia, with experienced military men both as *first* and second in command, would conduce more to the public good, than the existing divided corps at the civil lines and the cantonments. I therefore resigned the command in favour of Major Prendergast.

I retained the charge of the defences at Candaharee Bagh.

I sent my address to Mr. Harington, who wrote, "I am sure the men will be much pleased with it" (the address). "I will explain to Mr. Colvin the circumstances under which you have relinquished the command of your gallant little band, and can have no doubt that he will again thank you for the good service which you have rendered to the state, and applaud the public spirit by which you have been actuated throughout."

The Lieutenant-Governor, in the course of the month, honoured me and Major Prendergast by an official acknowledgment of our services. I regret to add that disease, brought on by fatigue and exposure, ere long hurried Major Prendergast into an untimely grave. He died, like many others who had been exposed to excessive heat and hard work, from cholera, soon after our retirement to the Fort. Courteous, prudent, and brave, no officer was more popular, and more justly respected by his men. After his death, Mr. Vere, a spirited gentleman in the customs department, was placed in charge of the corps, with a Lieutenant's commission. It was still doing good service when I left Agra.

During the latter half of the month of June, Colonel Fraser, Mr. Harington, and the Judges of the Sudder Court, had occasion to remonstrate very earnestly with the Lieutenant-Governor with regard to his policy. I have already hinted that the Police at Agra, as at other places in the North-Western Provinces, was more feared than respected by most men who wished well to the British Government. In the first place, all over Upper India, every man who had a pretension to an uniform, who knew any thing of drill or a firelock, set himself up for a Sepoy. Now, the Agra Police not only were dressed, drilled, and armed, but also had an enormous supply of balled ammunition served out to them by the Magistrate, the Honourable Robert Drummond. This gentleman, in the early days of the revolt, had acquired the confidence of all men, by his courage, zeal, and activity. But, as time wore on, and matters assumed a graver complexion, he, Englishman like, fell into the same error which I have attributed to the military officers of Gwalior. Nothing could shake his faith in his men. Unfortunately these men — I mean his leading and confidential agents—were all, without exception, Mahomedans, and the Mahomedans were all, or nearly all, traitors thirsting for English blood.—So it happened that at Agra we found ourselves in the hands of a Magistrate who was himself, as we all thought, victimized by a clique of cunning blood-thirsty Mahomedans. The high spirit and courage of Mr. Drummond gave weight to his counsels, his position as Magistrate of Agra gave him opportunity. He alone could, under our constitution, *act:* his superiors, with the exception of Mr. Colvin, having only the power to protest or expostulate. His principle was to show no sign of fear, and he considered every precaution to be a sign of fear. The Lieutenant-Governor, worn out by incessant fatigue, depressed by daily tidings of disaster, the victim of approaching disease, put himself, I may almost say entirely, into Mr. Drummond's hands. High-minded, frank, and open, he naturally preferred to trust men rather than suspect them. He trusted Drummond, as under ordinary circumstances he might well do, and Drummond trusted his Mahomedan subordinates, whose object was to destroy him and every other Englishman in Agra. At the invitation of the Police, as was generally believed, the whole of the mutineers from Neemuch, horse and foot, with a powerful artillery, were marching steadily upon us. The Police cut off our communications, opposed the officers who were engaged in victualling the Fort, and by their insolent demeanour, daily proved more plainly what was passing in their minds.

Colonel Fraser, Mr. Harington, Mr. Vansittart,

my colleagues, and I, watched their proceedings with anxiety, and remonstrated with the Lieutenant-Governor. We felt convinced that when the Neemuch mutineers attacked the Station, the Police would cut off the retreat to the Fort, and we urged, not that we ourselves should be admitted, nor even our wives and families, but that the schools, the convents, the old and infirm, and those who were too poor to have any vehicle, should be allowed to take up their quarters within the walls of the Fort. For ourselves, we determined to hold the Candaharee Bagh to the last moment, and most of the ladies of the Civil Lines, with their children and nurses, slept there every night.*

It was not till the end of the month that Mr. Colvin consented to allow the helpless part of the Christian population to retire within the Fort. It was forbidden to send in any property beyond the sort of allowance which a French Customs House Officer at Calais or Marseilles, passes under the term of a *sac de nuit.*† Hence, the loss and destruction of books, furniture, archives, records, public and private, and the ruin of hundreds of families. This loss might have been avoided, if in the beginning of the mutiny, as at Lahore, precautions

* Thanks to Mr. Morgan's kindness, every woman and child was welcome. The garden was filled with tents, in which, as well as in the house, the women and children slept, whilst the men took their share of the duty as sentries, &c.

† This prohibition was slightly relaxed when almost too late to benefit the public. Boxes were admitted on a written order from the officer in charge of the Fort.

had been taken at once. Our truest courage was to be prepared for the worst. I am not aware that any precautions could eventually have saved our houses at Agra from destruction, but invaluable property might have been preserved, if early permission had been given to place it within the precincts of the Fort. The work of victualling might have proceeded at one gate, whilst private and public property was admitted at another.

CHAP. VI.

THE RETIREMENT TO THE FORT.

THE month of July had set in. Colonel Fraser, considering the Candaharee Bagh no longer tenable, had left us, and taken a small house under the walls of the Fort. Residents in Cantonments looked at us in the Civil Lines, as doomed men. The fine frame of Mr. Colvin was sinking under the ravages of disease, yet he persisted in attending to every detail of business; whilst he acknowledged to me that the load of responsibility, the agony caused by the sufferings and dangers of his officers at every station in Upper India, was too much for human endurance, he resolutely watched every detail of public business. Even now, if I wanted a sword or a pistol from the magazine, Mr. Colvin's counter-signature was necessary.

His cares might well press hard on the strongest frame. The fabric of Government was falling to pieces, all over the North-Western Provinces. High officials, accustomed to command the obedience of millions, were hiding in the jungles, hunted by their own guards, or holding desperate positions against hopeless odds. One cry for help arose from east to west. Vibart and Robert Thornhill, at

Furuckabad,* with a score of men armed with fowling pieces, were defying whole regiments, keeping thousands at bay; Major Raikes and John Powel holding out against hope at Mynpoorie. Probyn, the Magistrate of Furuckabad, hidden in the hut of a friendly Zemindar. Cocks, Watson, young Harington, and a dozen English gentlemen at Allygurh, with mutineers on every side of them. In Rohilcund, Rajpootana, Cawnpore, and Bundelcund silence, too often the silence of the grave. At Futtehpore, Robert Tucker defending himself single-handed against the villains whom he had refused to suspect, and dying only when his last bullet was expended. And so all over the country, the English were at bay. Mr. Colvin expected much from his subordinates, but he had a heart to feel for their sufferings. He could not bear to give up station after station to anarchy, neither could he quietly see his trusted friends and officers butchered like sheep. The struggle consumed him. "The wrath of God is upon us," he exclaimed, "if we retire into the Fort."

Nevertheless, early in July events hurried on, which drove Mr. Colvin and every other living Christian, man, woman, or child at Agra, and within a radius of a hundred miles round about, into the Fort, glad enough to lose their property, and seek the only shelter for life now remaining. Mutiny, like a belt of fire, surrounded us.

* The scraps in French which we used to get from Furuckabad asking for help, which Mr. Colvin was unable to give, were heartrending.

Still we held in Agra a straggling position, from east to west some six miles long, with only one regiment of European soldiers, and a few undisciplined militia. Each day brought the Neemuch mutineers nearer. Regiments or detachments, hitherto faithful, were reported one after the other in mutiny. To bring our dangers to a climax, the Joudpore Legion, consisting of some two thousand men of all arms, were ordered into the Station just as the Neemuch mutineers arrived within a couple of marches of Agra. This last move brought matters to a crisis. I asked the opinion of Major M'Leod, Military Secretary to the Lieut.-Governor, and Captain Nixon, who had just come in to Government House from Bhurtpore, as to whether we in the Civil Lines, in the immediate vicinity of the Jail, with its four thousand desperadoes, and four miles from the Cantonments, could safely keep our wives and children there any longer. The answer was,—No. Thus, about the last day of June, we took the women and children to the Fort, to exchange their spacious and well-furnished houses for any hut that might be allotted them. I felt it a relief to see them comparatively safe, but the ladies themselves begged to be allowed to stay out with us, and to continue to share our dangers at Candaharee Bagh. Here I pause to offer a tribute of admiration to the courage and endurance of our English women. Throughout the mutiny self seemed forgotten, anxieties, if vented, were only for the husband, the brother, or the friend.

Up to the 4th of July, with Mr. Harington and

my colleagues, I continued to sleep outside the Fort. On the night of the 3rd, we held our last watch at the Candaharee Bagh. Restless and sleepless, from a fever which had for some time past been progressing upon me, I watched the sleepers around. There lay the member for Agra, of the Legislative Council of India, half dressed, a sword by his bed side, a gun in the corner, and a revolver under his pillow. Those gaunt, unshaven, weary-looking men by his side are the Judges of the Sudder Court. For six weeks they have been watching the rising flood of revolt, which had now risen more than breast high. Will they ever sleep with a roof of their own over their heads again?

On the 4th, we all spent part of the day in the Fort. I was prostrate with fever, and unable to lift up my head. The forms of office went on, and though the Court was closed and I had no home to go to, save a barrack in the Fort, I considered it right to obtain a regular certificate of my condition.*

Owing to my illness, I am unable to report the occurrences of the 4th as an eye-witness. I remember, however, that my cousin, Major Raikes, who had just come in from Mynpoorie, his men in the eleventh hour having deserted him, went to Mr. Colvin, or the Brigadier, or both, with my

* "I hereby certify that Mr. Raikes, C.S., is suffering from an attack of fever, for which I have prescribed, and I consider it necessary that he should remain quiet at home for a few days.

"S. CLARK, Assistant Surgeon.

"July 4th, 1857."

hearty concurrence, to urge that the Joudpoor Legion should be at once disarmed. No reasonable man could doubt that they would take the first favourable moment to turn upon us, and the mutineers from Neemuch were already almost within sight of Agra. In the afternoon of the 4th, the Legion broke into mutiny, murdered the European Sergeant-Major, and went off to join the Sepoy army, now within a few miles of Cantonments. The Lieutenant-Governor, who for some weeks past had spent the nights in Cantonments, came into the Fort. The Civil Lines were by this time nearly deserted. All held their breath, intent upon the coming struggle, when the fate of Agra was to be decided.

It is no part of my intention to chronicle battles. Every one knows that on the 5th July, Brigadier Polwhele led out his men to attack the mutineers, that after a hard fight he retired into the Fort surrounded by clouds of the enemy's cavalry, whilst their infantry and artillery moved off in the opposite direction towards Muttra and Delhi.

The Brigadier has been blamed; I presume because he was not successful. For all this, he was a true soldier. We have time now to consider the difficulties of his position. And who can deny that they were overwhelming? In the first place he considered it his duty to obey implicitly Mr. Colvin, who had been invested with the powers of the Governor-General. He carried out a policy in the matter of the preparation of the Fort, for instance, to which he himself was opposed. He might possibly have resisted more earnestly, on this and other points, the wishes of the Lieutenant-Governor, but he is not justly obnoxious to the sort of blame which has been lavished on him, merely because he feared, in a time of military convulsion, to throw overboard the Civil Government. His difficulties were enormous. It early became evident that contingents, legions, levies, every sort of military organisation, except the personal guards of Scindia, would join their Sepoy brethren and turn against us. The more troops we had, save our one weak European regiment and battery, the greater our danger. A powerful enemy threatened us from without; treachery grew up within and around us. The Mahratta guards were withdrawn.

Brigadier Polwhele determined to strike a blow at the enemy, with 500 men against 5000. He struck and failed. He could not command success, but I should be sorry to say that he did not deserve it.

Owing to my rank in the service, I was allowed to occupy one of the best quarters in the Fort, in the tiled barracks. We had three rooms, each about fourteen feet square. No windows, but a wooden door to each, and a veranda on either side. Our party, besides Mrs. Raikes and myself, consisted of two families, the Reverend Valpy French, his wife and two children; Major Raikes, Mrs. Raikes and one child: there were also two wet-nurses, and three women servants. One room served for the gentlemen at night, and for our dining-room at day. The other two rooms were given up to the ladies and children. It was hot and uncomfortable, as may be supposed, but not intolerable. We put up punkahs, and hired little native Christian boys to pull them. Many of our friends had much more confinement to bear.

From my sick bed in the afternoon of Sunday, the 5th July, I heard the cannonade, which lasted for nearly two hours. There was a commotion in the veranda, and my wife came in to tell me that Mr. French, who had watched the battle from the ramparts, reported our discomfiture. The English, surrounded by clouds of cavalry, were retreating slowly towards the Fort, ever and anon facing and firing volleys at their pursuers.

Then came the rush of weary soldiers to the Canteen, which was close to our room, and in the same barrack. Bloody, thirsty, covered with dust and smoke, the soldiers clamoured for drink. Beer, tea, wine and water were hastily given them by the ladies of our party. I could overhear their remarks. "Ah my chummie! my townie!" said one, whose comrade had been left dead on the battle field. "Faith! and the Major (Major Thomas) went at 'em grand," said another. The long string of hospital litters passed through the Fort gates. The gallant D' Oyley was carried in to die. Young Williams was undergoing the amputation of a leg in the hospital. Richard Oldfield, Under-Secretary to Government, was brought faint, and steeped in blood, to his young wife. I had a small tent near the barrack; in this two wounded officers were lodged.

A line of fire in the Cantonments showed the course of the retreating enemy. Barracks, private houses, bazaars, all were in a blaze.

On the 6th and 7th July, our tired men were not allowed to leave the Fort. My own house and a large part of the Civil Lines were not burnt until after the night of the 6th. Then the natives, who had hitherto protected our property, seeing that we did not leave the Fort, gave us up. The King of Delhi was proclaimed in the public places, and every remaining house was burnt and plundered. Few servants were to be found, we had to draw water from the wells inside the Fort, and were badly supplied with food. But all this passed away when, on or about the 8th, a military demonstration was made, and some guns and infantry marched through the city. At once there was a reaction. The people flocked to the Fort with provisions; washermen, water-carriers, tailors, shepherds, cooks and sweepers came pouring in to help their masters, who were generally too glad to see their domestics to ask many questions as to how the days since the 5th had been passed.

I, for one, do not blame these men for retiring quietly out of the fray, and standing aloof at a moment when it would have been certain death to them to pursue any other course. If they came near the Fort, our soldiers fired at them; if they showed at a distance from the Fort any disposition to help the Christians, the mutineers and Mahomedan rabble would have murdered them at once.

Some few servants, generally Mahomedans, behaved ill, and joined with the prisoners and rabble in the plunder of their masters, but most of the menial class continued faithful. On my own establishment, one old and favoured servant, a Mahomedan butler, behaved ill amongst about fifty. The rest were singularly devoted and faithful, and followed me in all my subsequent wanderings up to the Punjab and down to Calcutta.

CHAP. VII.

LIFE IN THE AGRA FORT.

THREE miles from the Civil Lines, and one mile from Cantonments, on a gentle curve overhanging the right bank of the river Jumna, stands the Fort of Agra: with its high red sandstone walls, deep ditch, and drawbridge, it looks now—what it really was when the Emperor Akber rebuilt it in 1570—impregnable.

Within are the Palace, with its gilded cupolas, and rich tracery of gold and blue enamel, on which Akber lavished millions; the Motee Musjid, or Pearl Mosque, of pure marble, and dazzling whiteness; the Arsenal, and other public buildings. Such is the Fort of Agra. When visiting the Palace or the Motee Musjid in happier days, how little had any sight-seeing Englishman expected that within those walls the shattered remnants of his nation would one day be crowded?

Yet so it was. Whatever remained unscathed, from Meerut to Allahabad, either of Englishmen or of their works, was conglomerated here. Here were the remnants of the record of survey and revenue settlement, that great work on which heaps of money and the best energies of our best men had been lavished for a quarter of a century. Here were the only munitions of war, the only instruments of art or materials of science, which remained to us.

In huts hastily prepared, amongst the galleries and gateways of the old Palace of the Emperors, a motley crowd assembled. Matted screens were set up along the marble corridors which in Akber's time were hung with the silks of Persia and the brocades of Benares.

Under this shade not only was every part of our British Isles represented, but we had also unwilling delegates from many parts of Europe and America. Nuns from the banks of the Garonne and the Loire, priests from Sicily and Rome, missionaries from Ohio and Basle, mixed with rope dancers from Paris, and pedlars from Armenia. Besides these we had Calcutta Baboos, and Parsee merchants. Although all the Christians alike were driven by the mutinous legions into the Fort, the circumstances of the multitude were as various as their races.

There were men who had endured more than all the afflictions of Job, who had lost like him not only their sons, daughters, and every thing they possessed, but who also mourned over the fate of wife, mother, and sister! Reserved, silent, solitary amongst the crowd, they longed either to live alone with their grief, or to quench the fire within by some hurried act of vengeance or despair.

Some few there were, on the other hand, who secretly rejoiced in the troubles of the Christian race, who fattened on their spoil and waited only to betray them if opportunity should offer.

The mass had lost their property: the householder his houses, the merchant his money, the shopkeeper his stores. Part, however, was saved: you could buy millinery or perfumery, but not cheese, beer, wine, nor tobacco.

In short, we had to rough it at Agra, to bear discomfort and privation; but as the bazaars soon opened and generally remained open, we had no real hardships to undergo. If our army retired from before the walls of Delhi, or if the Gwalior Contingent, with their artillery and siege train, made up their minds to attack us, as was constantly threatened, then we might be subjected to a siege. Havelock wrote us that he hoped to come soon; in the meantime, added he, "let Agra be as Julalabad."

Early in September, Mr. Colvin asked me to prepare a plan for the restoration of the Police in the North-Western Provinces, and I submitted a note on the subject; on the 7th, I called to talk over the matter, but found the Lieutenant-Governor too ill to attend to business. On Wednesday, 9th, to our great sorrow he died, and on the next day, I, as pall bearer, paid my last tribute of respect to his memory. After ruling over the fairest provinces of India in her palmiest days, he died without secure possession of an acre of ground beyond the Fort, and his body was interred within the walls—an abler pen than mine has done justice to his public and private character. I will merely repeat what I have said already. He perished, because in spite of the entreaties of his friends, he would persist in continual mental labour, when his physical state demanded complete repose. The Governor-General paid a just tribute to his name and memory.*

On the 13th September, Major Raikes' child died. She had been snatched by her mother from the bayonets of the Gwalior soldiers, and, I think, had never recovered from the exposure of the journey from Gwalior to Agra.

My own health, too, broken by an insidious fever, long since contracted in the Punjab, entirely failed, and my medical advisers expressed their opinion that a change to an European climate was necessary.

Here I resume my journal.

"*September* 18*th.*—Noon. A message from a banker at Khoorja to another at Hatrass as follows:—

"'Company's rupees are current in Delhi City, though not in the Fort. Two thousand Lucknow rupees received here, and will be sent to Coel† to-morrow.' The meaning of this cautiously worded despatch was clear enough. The English had got into the city of Delhi, and some of the mutineers had run as far as Khoorja." ‡

* See "Calcutta Gazette Extraordinary." Notification, dated 19th September, 1857.

† Allygurh.

‡ A town on the grand trunk road, between Delhi and Allygurh.

From Delhi also, came other mutineers along the right bank of the Jumna, in vast numbers, to Muttra. There they divided; part went across the river by a bridge of boats, which they constructed, and marched towards Furuckabad. Others struck across, in a south-westerly direction, to Dholpore, and, combining with some of the Gwalior Contingent and other rebels and mutineers, decided to attack Agra.

I take up my journal again.

"*September* 21*st.*—To-day, the news from Delhi is decidedly good. We took the magazines and vast stores, including 120 guns, on the 16th, and are gradually taking the city. The Gwalior accounts are better. I feel, for the first time, as if we might, without presumption, look forward with some confidence to the future.

"*October* 3*rd.*—The mutineers are leaving Muttra.

"*Wednesday*, 7*th.*—The mutineers from Dholpore are moving in this direction with heavy guns.

"*Thursday*, 8*th.*—Last evening, Major Montgomery was ordered in with his detachment. He has done excellent service between this and Allygurh. He is much disgusted that Colonel Fraser (who has been appointed to act as Chief Commissioner, with full civil and military authority) will not allow him, with about 150 men and two guns, to attack the mutineers, who have some 10,000, and ten or twelve guns. We hear that Greathed's column will be here by Saturday.

"*Saturday*, 10*th.*—We went to the Shah

Boorj (Royal Bastion) this morning, to see Colonel Greathed's moveable column cross the bridge. Sikhs, lancers, three batteries of horse artillery, and the skeletons of two Queen's regiments. This column came in by long forced marches, owing to an express sent out by Colonel Fraser. From the bastion we went down to the Delhi Gate. The Queen's 8th passed within three yards of us. 'Those dreadful-looking men must be Afghans,' said a lady to me, as they slowly and wearily marched by. I did not discover they were Englishmen until I saw a short clay pipe in the mouth of nearly the last man. My heart bled to see these jaded miserable objects, and to think of all they must have suffered since May last, to reduce fine Englishmen to such worn, sun-dried skeletons. 'Sure, your honour,' said an Irish serjeant, 'and it's the air has been too strong for 'em; they was well enough in Delhi amongst the stink, but coming out into the fresh country air has been too much for 'em.' I did not argue the point, but thought that the damp nights and hot days, with long marches and constant fights, had probably done more harm to the poor fellows than the 'fresh country air.' They wore the Khakee, or dust-coloured Sikh Irregular uniform. We tried to follow the column in the carriage, but found such a stoppage from baggage near the Umur Singh Gate, that we turned back. Just after breakfast garrison orders came, Militia Rifles to march out towards Dholpore in the afternoon, with the 3rd Europeans. On seeing this, I went over to the

Chief Commissioner, to ask whether he would like me to go out with them, or not.* He desired me to stay in the Fort. As I left Colonel Fraser a serjeant stepped up, saluted and said, 'Our camp is attacked.' Guns were heard, I went up to the ramparts, saw two of the enemy's tumbrils explode; then a line of dust as our cavalry and artillery charged and pursued the flying enemy."

I put down my journal here to describe more fully the events of the day. Soon the wounded began to come in. The hospital clothes which Mrs. Raikes (at Dr. Farquhar's request) had prepared, were most valuable; indeed, as Colonel Fraser said, they could not have provided for the wounded without the Civil Hospital clothing made up by Mrs. Raikes, and the ladies of Agra.†

Bleeding, lacerated, burnt and contused, the sufferers were carried into the "Motee Musjid," or Pearl Mosque. In this "Marble Temple," the most graceful building in Asia, rough wooden cots were hastily prepared, the mattrasses, pillows and quilts, which the ladies in the Agra Fort had so long been making, were soon in full demand. Here, covered with wounds, many of which seemed mortal, was carried the gallant Captain Jones ‡, of

* I belonged not to the Militia, but to a Rifle Company for the defence of the Fort.

† The Government gave the cloth, and the ladies made up the various articles of hospital clothing. They were intended for the Civil Hospital in the event of a siege, which happily never took place.

‡ He recovered with the loss of an eye.

Her Majesty's 9th Lancers. Younghusband* too came in, surrounded by his faithful Sikh soldiers, who had dragged him out of the well into which he, horse and all, with two or three men on the top of him, had fallen, whilst pursuing the flying Sepoys. Ere long the spacious corridors were filled with sick and wounded men. Dr. Farquhar requested Mrs. Raikes to preside over the hospital arrangements. Of her labours, and of those of many ladies who, with her, soothed and tended the sufferers, I will say not another word. But, I must describe the conduct of the British soldier in the day of sickness and pain. For weeks that the ladies † watched over their charge, never was a word said by a soldier which could shock the gentlest ear. When all was over, and when such of the sick and wounded as recovered were declared convalescent, the soldiers, in order, as they expressed it, to show their gratitude for the kindness of the ladies, modestly asked permission to invite their nurses and all the gentry and society of Agra to an entertainment in the beautiful gardens of the Taj. There, under the walls of the marble mausoleum,

* Lieut. Younghusband would not stay to be cured, but went in with Col. Greathed, and was killed when with Sir Colin Campbell, in the advance on Furuckabad.

† The ladies were divided into watches, and attended day and night. To avoid teasing the men by too much nursing, they were in a small separate room, and, *at stated periods*, went round to give tea, jelly, soda water, coffee, soup, or to help in dressing the wounds of the patients. All was done under the orders of the medical officers.

amidst flowers and music, these rough veterans, all scarred and mutilated as they were, stood up to thank their countrywomen who had clothed, fed, and visited them, when they were sick. Every lady in Agra was ready to join in this good work, and not one of them but will bear testimony to the delicacy of feeling and conduct, as well as the hearty gratitude, of these brave men.

To return to our immediate subject. The enemy who had surprised* our camp were thoroughly routed. Greathed began the attack; Cotton, the superior officer at Agra, took up and furiously pushed on the pursuit. The camp, guns, ammunition, and stores fell into our hands. I return to my journal.

"Evening.—Our men coming slowly in, quite done up. To relieve them we are to furnish guards to-night.

"*Sunday*, 11*th*.—Last night I mounted guard at the Umur Singh Gate. I was elected sergeant; Money†, corporal; Hugo James, and Wylly (Judge

* The surprise happened thus. The civil authorities, on the 9th October, urged Greathed to come in, as the reconnoitring party sent towards the enemy had been fired at and driven into Agra. But, on the morning of the 10th, the Magistrate and other Government officials assured Col. Greathed (as it had been reported to them) that the enemy had fallen back. *Hinc illæ lacrymæ.*

† Mr. Wigram Elliott Money, Commissioner of Customs for the North-Western Provinces. With much spirit he joined Mr. Harvey, the Commissioner of Agra, who, with a small party of Englishmen, penetrated nearly up to Delhi early in

of Agra) amongst my men. Thanksgiving for our victory offered in Church in the Marble Hall. Well may we be thankful! We had been shut up in this Fort of Agra since 5th July, and the enemy, always at hand, never made up their mind to attack us until a couple of hours after a strong column had marched into the place. We have taken their camp, treasure, thirteen guns, including one prodigious brass piece, and slaughtered heaps of the mutineers.

"*Friday*, 16*th*.—Re-writing memorandum on the Police, for the local Government.

"*Tuesday*, 20*th*.—Our Court had lately been sitting in the Fort. We have now taken rooms in the Custom House, and carry on work there.

"*Friday*, 23*rd*.—I have been appointed Special Commissioner under Section 7, Act XIV., of 1857, with authority to issue commissions under Section 2, Act XVII., with powers of life and death. John Lawrence writes from Lahore, 21st October:—'I assure you, when I look back on the events of the last four months, I am lost in astonishment that any of us are alive. But for the mercy of God we must have been ruined.

"'Had the Sikhs joined against us, nothing, humanly speaking, could have saved us. No man could have hoped, much less foreseen, that they would have withstood the temptation to avenge their loss of national independence.

June. Mr. Money's genial presence, on his return, rendered the Fort of Agra a very tolerable abode to his friends.

"'Even as matters now are it will be no ordinary task reconstructing the Administration, putting all things straight, getting rid of old abuses, avoiding former mistakes.

"'I often think and lament over the sad fate, the premature death, of George Christian,' &c. &c.

"There is only one opinion amongst us all here, and this I find was entirely shared by the officers from Delhi, that we owe our preservation, under God's blessing, to John Lawrence and Robert Montgomery, who strained every nerve, not only resolutely to keep order in the Punjab, but also to hurl every available soldier, European, or Sikh, against Delhi."

CHAP. VIII.

A VISIT TO DELHI AFTER THE SIEGE.

During the past nine months our four younger children had been with their Governess in the mountains at Landour. Some kind friends escorted them in safety to Agra, where they arrived on 23rd November. On the afternoon of that day, a few hours after our party had passed, a large body of mutineers, in arms, crossed the road by which they had been travelling. These men, the remnant of a mutinous army from Joudpore, had been beaten by our column under the late Colonel Gerard, at Narnol, in the Rewarree country, south-west of Delhi, and then had cut across the Jumna, some two thousand strong, with so much secrecy and despatch, that none of the authorities at Agra knew of their movements until they were actually across the road between Allygurh and Agra.

On the 15th December, finding the road to Cawnpore closed, I determined to take my family home viâ Bombay, passing through Delhi, Umballa, and Ferozpore, and thence proceeding in a country boat down the Indus to Kurachee.

I took a light camp equipage, and arranged to travel hastily through the disturbed districts by post, and from Delhi to make double marches, using my own horses and carriages. I took advantage of Brigadier Seaton's advance from Delhi towards Mynpoorie to hasten up in the wake of his force, and on the 16th, at dusk, we all reached Delhi in safety.

To return to my Journal:—

"*December* 17*th.*—Last night we slept in the old King's bed-room, after dining in what was his Zenana. This morning I went with Saunders to see the breach, the several points of attack and defence, and the posts we held during the memorable days of the siege. The ruined buildings, the trees cut and shorn of their boughs, the fragments of scattered shot and shell, all tell of the intense strife and rage of the conflict.

"During the day I spent an hour in the Marble Hall of Justice, where Brigadier Chamberlain was presiding over a Military Court assembled for the trial of the Nawab of Jhujar. At the commencement of the outbreak, instead of aiding the British officers, he treated them with contempt, lending a rupee to one and a grass-cutter's pony to another; whereas his ancestors had been raised to power by Lord Lake, and enjoyed a large territory from the British Government, on the express condition of aiding us with some four hundred horse. All his men joined the rebel army, his Fort was found fully stored with munitions of war, his Vakeels attended the rebel King of Delhi, &c., &c. After hearing his defence, it seems to me that he has behaved very badly and deserves punishment.

"In the evening we went again over the breach with Brigadier Chamberlain.

"*December* 18*th*.—We went to see the Jumma Musjid, which is held now by a battalion of Beloochees. I sincerely hope that the plan proposed by Mr. Philip Egerton, the Magistrate of Delhi, may be carried out.* He suggests that the Mosque be used henceforth as a Christian Church, and on each of the thousand compartments on the marble floor, the name of one of our Christian Martyrs be inscribed. It is the general opinion that it would be madness to restore this noble building to the Mahommedans.

"In the afternoon I had a long and very interesting walk with Major Reid, the hero who, with his noble little Goorkhas, held our advanced post at Hindoo Rao's house, from first to last, throughout the siege of Delhi. The courage, fortitude and devotion of these officers and men are beyond praise. The Goorkhas under Major Reid were the first natives to throw boldly their lot into ours, and to fight, Brahmin against Brahmin, Hindoo against Hindoo, on the English side. The anxiety with which these brave little Nepalese † were watched in

* I wrote to Sir John Lawrence, urging him to attend to this proposition; I have not heard the result.

† It is satisfactory to observe that the Nepalese are only formidable when under European training and led by English officers. Jung Bahadoor can make little of them; but men such as Fisher was, and Reid is, can lead Goorkhas anywhere and do any thing with them.

their first encounter was intense. The mutineers came out of Delhi and advanced towards the Goorkha post, calling out, 'You will not fire at us, we are all of one caste, we are your brothers and friends.' The Goorkhas made no demonstration until the Sepoys had come close up to them, when they greeted them with a volley, a cheer, and a rush, kookree in hand, which put all future ideas of fraternization out of the question.

"I walked over the ruins of Hindoo Rao's house with astonishment. How men could have held a building so battered and riddled with shot and shell, the very target of the enemy, is a marvel; yet as the siege progressed, when it was proposed to remove even the sick and wounded in hospital, they violently protested against being carried away from their comrades even to a place of safety. In this hospital Major Reid pointed out the mark where a patient had been cut in half by a round shot. After spending an hour or two on the heights, where the Major had been engaged in *twenty-five regular fights*, to say nothing of an incessant cannonade which went on day and night for months, we proceeded to the spot on the bridge over the canal in the suburb, where he fell on the morning of the assault, in his twenty-sixth engagement. He lost nearly all his little Goorkhas, and can with difficulty, if at all, replace them. He enlists only the fighting castes, and wonderful soldiers they are; the only men in India, so far as I know, who never drink, loot, nor run away. I had heard that when their leader was knocked over, the Goorkhas, unable to advance, and unwilling to retreat, sate down on the bridge under a shower of bullets. This Major Reid denies. He has a terrible gash in his head, and ought to be taken care of by Government, as he is not the sort of man to take care of himself.*

"19*th.* — We drove ten miles out of Delhi to spend the day at the country house of Sir Theophilus Metcalfe, near the Kootub Minar. It was a strange sight — a house full of books, pictures, and elegant furniture — in the middle of the mutineers' camp, or at least of the country overrun by them. I questioned the servants how they had managed to preserve their master's property intact, when not a stone belonging to any Christian was left standing all over the country. They answered evasively. My belief is that the King of Delhi had the place preserved for his own use, and considering the beauty of the house and grounds, he showed his good taste. I may here mention that I read several of the King's orders, written with his own pencil, and proving what an ungrateful old man he is. The English saved his family from the most cruel tyranny of the Mahrattas, gave them back royal rank, and bestowed an ample pension, yet this hoary-headed sinner orders all Christians to be murdered, &c. &c.

* I never saw Major Reid before I went to Delhi, and know merely what I have described of him here. I may therefore suggest how *invaluable* his services might be if he were employed to raise 10,000 Goorkhas, for distribution, not into separate corps, but into fifty different regiments, in the mode described in a future chapter.

"Amongst the papers one amused me. It was from a native officer at Meerut, and ran somewhat thus:—

"After compliments the writer informs the Asylum of the Universe that His Majesty's sway from Meerut to Cawnpore is complete. In the district of Bolundshuhr, however, a rebel, one Turnbull, is trying to create a disturbance. 'If your Majesty will send a detachment of your victorious troops, he will easily be put down.'

"'One Turnbull' meant Mr. George Turnbull, the former Magistrate and Collector of Bolundshuhr, now Judge of Meerut. He, with Mr. Sapte, exerted himself to maintain order in the country, and thus obtained the distinction of being denounced as a 'rebel' to the King. Yesterday we all went, a large party of ladies and gentlemen, with Mr. and Mrs. Saunders, to see the King. He is a withered old man of ninety. I found him propped up with cushions on a bed, in a small house which formerly was occupied by a humble follower. I sat down on a chair by his side*, heard him rambling on about his dreams and quoting some verses of his own composition, and then left without addressing him. The ladies saw the Queen; she was in a very bad humour, and grumbled at having insufficient fuel. The King

* As a proof of the sensitive temper of the time, I may mention that I saw an account of this interview in an English newspaper, in which the writer expressed his surprise and disgust that I took off my hat when I entered the house in which the old King was.

has ten personal attendants, which seems a full allowance for a man who has only one room to live in. I have been reading the papers connected with the old King's capture. His life was guaranteed by Hodson, under the authority of General Wilson, *in order to prevent his escape.* Saunders had nothing whatever to do with it.

"In the evening I went out with General Penny on his elephant, to see the side streets of the city. For miles not a creature save a half-starved cat, and here and there an old hag groping about amidst the bones, old papers, and rags with which this once wealthy and populous place is strewed. It is as a city of the dead.

"Saunders* is working here as Commissioner ably and successfully, and as hospitable as ever."

* My first acquaintance with Mr. Charles B. Saunders was at Amritsur, in 1852. It was on the occasion of Sir Henry Lawrence's departure from the Punjab. One sample, the first I had, of Mr. Saunders' hospitality, will suffice. He had filled his house and grounds with friends to that degree that he and Mrs. Saunders were living in a tent pitched *on the top of the house*, in very inclement weather. As Deputy Commissioner of Amritsur, Mr. Saunders won all hearts. The old Sikh chiefs really adored him. Driven from Moradabad, where he was Magistrate, early in June, by the mutiny of the 29th N. I., he did excellent service in the country between Kurnal and Delhi, and accompanied our troops in the storm and gradual advance upon that city. Mild yet courageous, gentle yet firm, he has that rare mixed character of decision and suavity which is now beyond all price in India.

CHAP. IX.

FROM DELHI TO UMBALLA.

From Agra to Delhi we had travelled post, as it was considered on all hands imprudent to march with ladies and children on that road. It was a great delight to us all once more to find ourselves sufficiently far from mutineers of all sorts, to be able with a slight escort to avail ourselves of our tents, and we marched with comfort from Delhi to Umballa.

Our friend Mr. Robert Montgomery, the present Chief Commissioner of Oude, arranged to meet us on our journey to Ferozpore, and we were here looking forward to a pleasant voyage down the Indus to Bombay.

At Umballa, however, I received a letter from Mr. Jackson, late officiating Chief Commissioner of Oude, informing me, that having met with a severe accident (a broken leg) on the retreat from Lucknow, he was unable to accompany Sir Colin Campbell further, that His Excellency had written to Colonel Fraser, the Chief Commissioner at Agra, for my services, and had requested him to propose to me to accompany him on his advance from Cawnpore to Furuckabad and Mynpoorie, &c. The duty required was "to superintend the introduction of order, the re-establishment of our Government in the provinces from which Sir Colin had expelled the mutineers, and the punishing the insurgents." It was further notified to me that it was considered of "vital importance to the interests of Government that military successes should be immediately followed by the introduction of an efficient police, &c. &c." As Sir Colin Campbell and Mr. Jackson agreed in thinking it desirable that I should thus attend upon His Excellency, I accepted the invitation, and here subjoin copies of two letters written by me on the 26th and 27th of December, which will explain my proceedings better than any detail I can now give.

"*To Colonel Fraser, C.B., Chief Commissioner at Agra.*

"MY DEAR FRASER,

"Mr. Money writes me word that Sir C. Campbell had expressed to you, his wish that I should be deputed to his camp.

"I have no letters from you, or from your secretary on the subject, but I think it my duty in these times, to express my readiness to wait upon His Excellency.

"I have not yet formally and officially notified my acceptance of the leave granted me, and you may easily cancel my application.

"Sick and worn out as I am, I still would accompany the army as long as I had a leg to stand upon, and I might be, with God's blessing, of some use to my country. At all events, I cannot neglect such an invitation, and I await here your permission to join the camp at once.

"Write, if you please, to Mr. Saunders at Delhi, and he will telegraph your instructions to me.

"Your's, very sincerely,

"C. RAIKES."

To Sir Colin Campbell I wrote thus:—

"SIR,

"I have this day received a letter from Mr. Jackson, dated 13th December, in which he informs me that your Excellency has applied for my services, to attend your Camp.

"I had heard this from a private friend a day or two ago, and at once wrote to Colonel Fraser to request him to express to you my desire to wait upon you.

"My health is not strong, but I hope that I may be able to arrange such details of the Civil Administration as may be committed to my charge, and that completed, I shall hope to proceed to England with my family.

"I shall feel deeply mortified if Colonel Fraser should object to my accepting the duty for which your Excellency has been pleased to nominate me. It is one of which any Englishman might be proud, and I feel sensible of the honour done to me.

"I have, &c.,

"C. RAIKES.

"Camp, Umballa: 27th December, 1857."

I also wrote to General Mansfield, Chief of the

Staff, to say that if any other civil officer had been deputed, owing to my absence from Agra, I nevertheless claimed the right of serving Sir Colin. Not to quote other letters, I may here give the General's reply. Kind it is and courteous, like every communication which I received from him or Sir Colin:—

"6 A.M., January 3rd, 1858.
"Camp Kurowlie, three miles beyond left bank Kalee Nuddee.

"MY DEAR SIR,

"I have this morning received your letter of the 30th ultimo and shown it to His Excellency. He will be delighted to see you, and has not heard as yet of any deputation of another civilian by the Agra Government.

"Should he do so, nothing will permit interference with the arrangement respecting yourself, proposed for your consideration through Mr. Jackson.

"The garrison of Futtehgurh tried to defend the suspension bridge over the Kalee Nuddee, or rather attacked our working party employed in the repair of it, and compelled us to engage them. They lost all their guns and a few hundred men killed. Our loss was trifling.

"We advance close up to Futtehgurh to-day.

"I am, &c.,

"W. MANSFIELD."

Pending a reply to my letters to Agra and the Head-quarters Camp, I paid a visit to the Maharaja of Putialee. This powerful Chief had rendered such important services to the British

Government during the campaign against the mutineers at Delhi, that I was anxious, on behalf of the Agra Government, to express my acknowledgments. After a visit of some days to Putialee, I can more than ever enter into the feelings of aversion with which our ablest officers regard any further annexation of native States. I can conceive no greater crime, nor any more extravagant political blunder, than it would be to annex such a principality as this of Putialee. To say that the subjects of this State are as contented and happy as those in our own conterminous districts is not enough. They get, I believe, cheaper and speedier justice than their near neighbours at Paniput did under the late Agra régime. They are, if anything, better fed, clothed, and housed than our own subjects; and, what is no small matter, they are, so long as we leave them alone, *on our side.* In order to cement the existing good feeling between us and native independent or protected States, we might well assure them, for the future, that even in the event of a failure of direct heirs, we have no wish to assume charge of new territories. Our true strength is in the support and confidence of our native allies, not in any further increase of territory.

The Maharaja received me with great ceremony and splendour, and lodged all our party in the Motee Bagh, or Pearl Garden, a country residence, or rather a painted hall, surrounded by flowers and fountains. Here, leading me aside, he gave earnest warning of the dangers of too large a Sikh army.

"Wait, sir," said he, "until this excitement of victory, this surfeit of plunder, be over; wait till you mass large bodies of Sikhs in your cantonments, and then remember that I warned you of the danger." This conversation made the greater impression on me as confirming the views of Brigadier Chamberlain, who a few days before had said to me, "The Sepoys have waited a hundred years to mutiny, the Sikhs, if subject to like temptations, will not wait ten!" He also had received from the Raja of Jheend a similar warning. Making full allowance for the hereditary prejudice which these Rajahs, as Malwa* Sikhs, have against the Manjha† Sikhs, I yet consider that we must be careful how we handle our Sikh levies; but I shall return to this subject in a future chapter.

Mr. Douglas Forsyth, now Secretary to the Chief Commissioner of Oude, was, at the time of my visit to Umballa, the Deputy Commissioner of that District. From all that Mr. Forsyth told me, it appears perfectly certain that the Maharaja‡ assisted us most materially and zealously during the late troubles, and indeed it is not too much to say, that without his help the Umballa Cantonment would

* On the left bank of the Sutlej River.

† Between the Beas and Ravee, about Amritsur, &c.

‡ The Maharaja, though very manly and straightforward in his manners, is not free from some of the conceits of Asiatic diplomacy. "Tell me," said he quietly to Mr. Forsyth, "whether Mr. Raikes is sent here to criticise my conduct; I have done much to show my respect and to make him welcome; but if he wants to find fault with me I will try to do even more."

hardly have been preserved. At the end of May, or early in June, when summoned to the station, he came clad in a suit of mail, driving his own elephant like a true Indian warrior, and spared neither personal fatigue nor exertion to prove his zeal for the British Government and against the mutineers. I have before me a newspaper,* lithographed by the rebels during the time that our troops were before Delhi, and dated to correspond with our 23rd August, 1857. To give a brief extract of one of the leading articles will suffice:—

"PUNJAB.—Although it appears, by the report of travellers from Lahore, that the murder and destruction of the impure infidels has taken place, yet some eye-witnesses declare that they hold forts and may be seen moving about during the day-time, and in short they have not been so thoroughly swept away as, by the favour of God, has been the case to the eastward. Still there is not a question that the Government of the infidels is over in the Punjab and elsewhere. But they receive supplies from the Maharaja of Putialee, who above all ungrateful men, assists and supports them. Therefore, a force should be sent out against him," &c. &c.

Soon after our return from Putialee, orders came for me to join the army in the field; so I prepared at once to retrace my steps to Agra, and thence to proceed to Head-quarters at Furuckabad.

* This paper was taken when our troops entered the Palace at Delhi.

CHAP. X.

FROM UMBALLA TO SIR COLIN CAMPBELL'S CAMP AT FURUCKABAD.

On my return from Umballa towards Delhi and Furuckabad, I paid a visit to the Nawab at Kurnal. This man, whose house and land is on the high road between Umballa and Delhi, had very early to make up his mind either to join the chiefs around Delhi, who had forsaken their allegiance to the British Government, or to take his stand with us.

Mr. Le Bas, the Judge of Delhi, after undergoing the greatest peril, escaped from that city to Kurnal. Soon after his arrival, during the interval that preceded the advance of our troops from Umballa viâ Kurnal, and just as the defection became known, when we had no military force near Kurnal, and all men watched anxiously the conduct of each local chief, the Nawab of Kurnal came to Mr. Le Bas and addressed him to the following effect.

"Sir, I have spent a sleepless night in meditating on the state of affairs: I have decided to throw in my lot with yours. My sword, my purse, and my followers are at your disposal."

So well did he act up to the engagement thus made, that after the fall of Delhi a testimonial was put into his hand by Mr. Le Bas, equally honourable to both. As a mark of regard the Judge gave the Nawab his favourite horse*, and a letter of thanks for his public services.

Amongst other marks of devotion to our cause, the Nawab had raised a troop of one hundred horse, armed and equipped on the model of the Punjab Mounted Police Corps. I can speak for their efficiency, as some of these men escorted me, under a native officer connected with the Nawab, from Kurnal to Benares.

I consider the conduct of this Mahomedan nobleman to deserve special commendation, and I trust that he has received suitable reward. Other Mahomedan Talookdars no doubt professed loyalty, and in some instances did good service, but few so entirely identified themselves with the cause which in May 1857, was generally considered by the people the losing one. Many who have received great credit for loyalty, were mere watchers of the event —as polite to the mutineers as to us, or as the natives expressed it, "*keeping their feet in both stirrups.*" My old friend at Kurnal was an honourable exception, he made no sort of parade of his services, and his only complaint when I saw him was, that we were far too gentle and generous to

* An animal of rare beauty and value, whose speed had saved his master's life in the flight from Delhi. I have these particulars from the Nawab, as I am not personally acquainted with Mr. Le Bas. But as I saw that gentleman's letters and the horse, I can trust to the general correctness of the information given me by the Nawab.

rebels in general, and to his own rebellious neighbours in particular.

After leaving my wife and family at Meerut, I proceeded viâ Agra, to take charge of my new duties with the Commander in Chief. At Agra I heard that the only remaining child of my late son-in-law, Mr. Christian, had, whilst a captive in the Palace at Lucknow, sunk under a disease brought on by bad food and confinement.

From this period up to the end of the month, I revert to my journal,—amplified as it is by some few papers which are inserted in order to throw light on the occurrences of the period.

"*Wednesday*, 13*th*.—Busy day at Agra. I went to speak to Dr. Farquhar.*

"All I could extort from him was, that he believed I was acting from a sense of duty, and so far right.

"*Thursday*, 14*th*.—Bought tents, brace of double-barrelled pistols, two horses. Hartigan† got me a first-rate Arab charger, when I was in despair of finding a good horse.

"Colonel Fraser wishes me to wait to go to the

* He had written to me thus on the 5th—"But a more important, because a public, consideration is, are you right in occupying such a post, with a shattered body; for, by all accounts, your duties will be more physical than mental. I heartily sympathise with your desire to serve, for I have applied to join the Field Hospital as soon as I am relieved here; but I should think I did wrong if I had not at present a *mens sana in corpore sano*."

† The sergeant of the 9th Lancers who made the speech about the lady nurses in the Taj.

Chief with a detachment of the Queen's 38th Foot here from Mynpoorie. I can't wait, and have ordered a relay of mail horses to be ready to take me to Mynpoorie, thence I must ride into camp with any escort I can get. Captain Bruce, who has just come in from head-quarters, has kindly lent me his tent there until my things come up.

"*Sunday*, 17*th*. — Head-Quarters Camp, Futty-gurh. I have had time to look about me. I started on Friday morning with Mr. Fullerton* in my travelling carriage. The first horse broke the shafts; however, we patched up the carriage and pushed on. The Mynpoorie folk seemed very glad to see me, and at Shekoabad and Ghurwur brought out some of the old 'ryklas' which they have been using against the mutineers, to fire a salute in my honour. What with their salutations and the complaints of '*be-duk-ilee*†' it was late before we reached Mynpoorie. We found the Magistrate, Mr. Boldero; my friend Chase his assistant, and the rest of the Civil Staff of the district, taking their supper in the old Sepoy guard-room attached to the Cutcherry‡; the Cutcherry itself being a

* The Reverend Mr. Fullerton is the devoted and excellent missionary of the American Presbyterian Mission at Agra. He went to gather his scattered flock at Furuckabad.

† Be-duk-ilee means dispossession. Thousands were forcibly dispossessed during the mutiny, and came praying for restitution the moment we resumed sway in our rural districts.

‡ Court house, in which the Magistrate-Collector transacts business, and the repository of the public records of the district.

heap of ruins, like every other English building in the place, the Church only excepted.*

"In the morning I received crowds of old friends, each anxious to declare his delight at having the 'sahib log' (gentlemen) back again. Balances of revenue coming in well. Sepoys in hiding in sugar cane fields all over the country, and abused by everybody.

"I took a melancholy walk over the station once so dear to me; saw my old house in ruins, the garden and lawn overgrown, tangled, and out of order; the Church-yard defaced, my serai lately used as a barrack for the rebel Rajah. Rao Bowannie Singh came to pay his respects: very civil, but I suspect him, and at best consider him but as a fair-weather friend.

"We drove to Bhowgong†, where, as the people knew I was coming, there was a great demonstration of loyalty. My poor Jemadar Balkishun had been killed here by the mutineers in May or June. I went into the Tuhseelee, one of the last public buildings constructed by me in 1852, before I left Mynpoorie for Lahore. The place had been occupied since July as a barrack by the rebel Rajah. Under the gateway were the scribblings of the mutineers on the wall—caricatures of the English,

* It is a curious fact that at Agra, Allygurh, Mynpoorie, Futtygurh, and other places, less damage was done to the Churches than to the private dwellings of the English.

† A large town, full of ill-conditioned Mahomedans, on the grand trunk-road, at the junction of the high-road to Agra *viâ* Mynpoorie.

with appropriate mottos, such as '*Maro Furingee*,' '*Furingee rota nye*,'* were scratched over the place. The Tehsildar of Bhowgong, who I presume had not noticed these hieroglyphics, looked very much ashamed when I suggested the expediency of a little whitewash. As I passed through the obsequious crowd outside (knowing the character of the people of this town), I could not help reflecting how different would have been my reception if Wilson at Delhi, and Sir Colin at Cawnpore and Furuckabad, had not vindicated the honour of our nation.

" At Bewur we mounted horses which the kindness of our friends at Mynpoorie had provided, and with an escort of five and twenty Mynpoorie Sowars pushed on towards Futtygurh. The sun was fast sinking as we approached within sight of the head-quarters camp.

" Sir Colin (who had just returned from an expedition to Walpole's brigade, which was watching the Ghat on the Ramfunga river, about ten miles from our camp across the Ganges in an easterly direction), received me with the utmost cordiality and kindness. I dined with him last night, meeting Sir David Baird, Lord Seymour, the two Alisons (one minus an arm), Major Metcalfe, Colonel Stirling, &c. &c.

" This morning I breakfasted with the Chief, and have since been to the staff mess tent to Church,

* Down with the English — the English are crying.

where the Rev. Mr. Mackie preached an excellent sermon.

"*Monday*, 18*th*.—I made the following note from information given me by an Italian gentleman, who has lately escaped from Lucknow.

"Mr. Steven Reghelini, a Catholic of Sirdhano, son of Major R. of the Begum Sumroo's service, a British pensioner of 200 rupees per mensem, went to Lucknow in search of some employment, and was in the city opposite the iron bridge living in a hired house, when the mutineers attacked Lucknow. He was protected, with Mr. Browne and several others, by Mirza Hatim Ali Beg, late Moonsiff of Chunar, and his son Sukawut Ali Beg, Mr. Gubbins's Moonshee, the last man to stay in the Residency, and who left with Mr. Gubbins's permission on the 30th of June. Mrs. Beale, wife of the Second Master of the Bareilly College, was one of the party saved by Sukawut Ali and his father. Mr. Reghelini relates of Lucknow thus:—

"'*Lucknow*.

"'Meerza Birjis Kudr Buhadoor is Sooba (or Viceroy) of Oude, under the King of Delhi, about twelve or thirteen years old. His mother is Huzrat Muhl. This boy is son of Wajid Ali Shah, the King of Oude, now prisoner in Calcutta.

"'Prime Minister Shurfoodowla, once Naib at Lucknow.

"'Momoo Khan, at Kaisar Bagh, Daroga of Dewan Khana Khanja.

"'Mujuffer Ali Khan, General, nephew of Shurfoodowla.

"'Ruhmut Oolla, Head Moonshee of Shurfoodowla.

"'Ahmud Ali, or Chota Mia, has charge of the magazine.

"'Maharaj Balkissan, Dewan.

"'Unwur Jee, Darogah of Vuzeer's Dewan Khana.

"'Ali Riza Beg, Kotwal, formerly Extra Assistant of Dureabad, under the British Government.

"'Ahmed Oolla Shah, Mahomedan leader, who came with the mutineers from Fyzabad. He was released from gaol; a regular rebel; was once in gaol in Agra. Through his example the troops take courage in the day of battle; he has been twice wounded.

"'*Artillery.*

"'Fyzabad Horse Artillery, six 6-pounders.

"'Colonel Gunge Ditto Ditto.

"'Nusseerabad Ditto nine guns.

"'A made up new battery, six guns.

"'Some guns left at Chinhut by Sir H. Lawrence; one large elephant gun.

"'Muchie Bowun guns, left by the British; two large rusty 24-pounders.

"'*Cavalry.*

"'300 Sowars. 15th Irregulars.

"'300 Ditto. 15th Recruits.

" ' 400 Sowars, 12th. — Fight well, Hurriana Ranghurs.

" ' 500 Ditto, under Moulvee Mustan Khan.

" ' 500 Ditto, under Sheikh Sookum.

" ' 300 Ditto, late Captain Daly's.

" ' A few of Hardinge's Russala.

" ' About 2000 troopers, Soobah's new levies, not well armed, badly mounted.

" ' *Infantry.*

" ' 1 Bohl ha pultun, from Fyzabad.

" ' 1 Bullum teer. (Volunteers.)

" ' 12 Police battalions.

" ' Some sappers and miners.

" ' 50 Regiments Nujeeb, some 100, some 200, in all about 10,000 men.

" ' 4000 Infantry Nusseerabad camp, from Delhi.

" ' *Petty Princes.*

" ' Raja Man Singh, with followers.

" ' „ Goorbucs Singh.

" ' „ Nawab Ali Khan.

" ' „ Benee Mallkoo.

" ' „ Lal Madhoo, of Kala Konkar.

" ' Chowdree Hushmut Ali, of Sundeela.

" ' Munsub Ali, of Russoolabad.

" ' In all about 200,000 men in arms in Lucknow alone.'

" Hodson came in from the Ram Gunga, where his horse are encamped with Walpole. He came, by order of Sir Colin, to inform me that certain Mahomedans in the vicinity of his camp had offered to assist, making no conditions for themselves whatever, and saying, that if any fault should hereafter be proved against them, they asked for no consideration; might he, asked Hodson, under the circumstances use them? I said, if these men offer without any condition to assist you, I can have no objection, and if you will send in their names and abode, I will tell you how far you may trust them.

"*Tuesday*, 19*th*.—Rode early to the City, Palace and Payeen Bagh; ordered up heaps of the rebel Duftur (record office), to be examined at leisure. I received letters from Government (Agra) with important communications as to the condition of the Meerut Division with respect to the Rohilcund insurgents. I took these papers over to Sir Colin, who very frankly stated his views to me, and promised to send on the documents with some pressing letters from the Magistrate of Etawah to Lord Canning.

"In addition to the public papers mentioned above, I placed before His Excellency the following private memorandum, written by one of the ablest Civil officers in the North Western Provinces, whose intimate knowledge of Rohilcund stamped value on every word:—

"'1. The Bijnore rebels are getting troublesome and bold. Small parties have crossed the Ganges; and, within the last few days, a larger body of 500 or 600 men—some say more—crossed, and burnt the Thaneh at Meeranpoor, in the south-east corner of the Moozufurnuggur district. They recrossed on our cavalry appearing. But the presence of 4000 or 5000 rebels, with guns, on the east bank of the Ganges, who are constantly threatening invasion, and are, doubtless, trying to stir up the disaffected against Government, has a bad effect on the district. Our troops are harassed with the duty of watching these rebels, and cannot do it effectually; and the sooner a column moves across and destroys the Bijnore rebels the better; for a slight mistake on our part, or a chance bit of success on theirs, might enable them to disturb the peace of the whole division to an extent that, with the few troops left here, would give serious trouble.

"'2. Further down the Ganges, opposite Anoopshahur, large parties of rebels are constantly threatening to cross, and firing on our people. They keep the district officers and all the troops constantly watching the bank of the river. The fact that, above and below, this occurs without any attempt to punish the rebels, is, to the people, proof of weakness.

"'3. It is well known that no reinforcements have reached this, and that troops have gone, and still continue to go—mounted and foot police are still constantly moving down—*from* this, and do not return; and the well wishers of Government on the east of the Ganges, who are earnestly begging for the advance of Government troops, report that the evil disposed on this side, are continually informing their friends, the rebels in Rohilcund, that no troops are left here, and inviting them to come over, and assuring them, if they will come, thousands and thousands will join them.

"'4. This is all talk, of course; but still it is talk that should be put a stop to without delay. The Nawab of Rampoor, who knows all that is going on in Rohilcund, has applied for the loan of eight 6-pounder guns, with ammunition, to enable him to resist the attacks which he declares will be made upon him if the reoccupation of Rohilcund is longer delayed.

"'5. This requisition, strongly seconded by the Commissioner of Rohilcund, has been submitted to the General of the Division, who cannot comply with it.

"'6. The Nawab—who has behaved in a most admirable manner—fears that, strengthened by the numbers of rebels driven from Oude by fear, and from Futtehgurh by our advance to that place, the Bareilly rebels will push up towards him. The inability to comply with his request for guns, and the non-appearance of any signs of an advance from this side, will greatly discourage him and all the well-wishers of Government, who, in the event of an influx of rebels and mutineers from the south-east, without any support from the west, will be exposed to great danger. If the rebels find the Upper Doab is not reinforced, their threats and attempts to cross will probably be matured into a serious combination with the smouldering disaffection, which has been suppressed but not eradicated.

"'7. In the meantime, the unfortunate Hindoos are being oppressed and plundered. A large amount of revenue is being exacted, which it would be hard to demand again from the people, who have been withholding it as long as they could, and begging for assistance; and while the revenue, already nearly all collected in the Upper Doab, is being rapidly expended, nearly fifty lacs of rupees, which might be got within the next three months in Rohilcund, and with which nearly all financial difficulties would disappear, are locked up when most urgently wanted.

"'8. Strong reasons in favour of an advance into Rohilcund from the west and north-west are indicated above.

"'9. With the exception of the rebels collected on the banks of the Ganges near Bijnore and Anoopshahur, who would be disposed of by columns of very moderate strength, there would be no opposition till the troops concentrated near Bareilly,—if then. The greater part of the Bijnore and Moradabad districts have been kept in order by the Nawab of Rampoor, who has his own people now at his beck. The force advancing from the north-west might be joined by 1000 Goorkhas, with four guns, now impatiently waiting at Huldewanee, below Nynee Tal, for permission to clear their front.

"'10. To the south and east of Bareilly, thousands upon thousands of Rajpoots are waiting, eager to take revenge for the oppression they have suffered for the last eight months, and to cut off all fugitives attempting to escape that way.

"'11. Every day the Rohilcund rebels near the Ganges are getting bolder, and the necessity for a speedy advance of troops to go into that province from the north-west side is becoming more urgent.'

"'Meerut: January 9th, 1858.'

"*Wednesday*, 20*th*.—An ordinary man might be perplexed at the confusion of interests and circumstances which invite Sir Colin's attention just now. The local Government at Agra, urging an immediate advance on Bareilly, and giving amongst other reasons the following:—

"The left bank of the Ganges, from the mountains right down to Sir Colin's front, swarming with Sepoys and Mahomedan rebels, with cavalry, infantry and artillery, continually threatening to cross the river, which is fordable at the present season; every now and then making a hasty rush across, swooping down to cut up some unfortunate outlying Police or Tehseel (revenue collection) station, to carry off if possible some luckless European telegraph signaller or patrol, and then recrossing the river to laugh at our beards. On the other hand come letters from the highest functionaries of State in Calcutta and elsewhere, pointing out the necessity of an immediate move upon Lucknow. The considerations which recommend both the advance upon Bareilly and the destruction of Lucknow, are momentous; in short it is obviously desirable and necessary to attack the enemy in both directions ere long, and, if possible, in both directions *at once;* but where are the troops to come from? No force that Sir Colin can collect will be more than enough to smash Lucknow, with its seven miles of buildings, two hundred thousand fighting men, as many more armed citizens, its powerful defences, artillery, &c. Sir Colin has represented to the Governor-General his own views, and now quietly awaits, like a true soldier, any orders that may be given.

"22*nd.* — The citizens affected to desire to illuminate Furuckabad, in honour of Sir Colin's occupation of the district. I say no; you have had too many English men and women murdered here; but if you wish to show your loyalty, let me see you support the British Government in every way by your conduct and influence. An attempt made to open communication with me by the rebel Queen at Lucknow.

"I brought to His Excellency's notice that the enemy had recrossed the Ganges, not twenty miles hence on our flank, and driven away our Police Thanah at Kaemgunge, and urged that he should give the civil power support; the Chief makes no promises.

"23*rd.* — I submitted for the consideration of the Commander-in-Chief this memorandum: —

"'One thousand rebels have crossed at Soorujpoer Ghat, opposite Kumpil. Nine thousand horse and foot, with nine guns, are preparing to cross, and getting a bridge ready.

"'They are said to be led by Mooltan Khan, of Mhow, near Kaemgunge. This is the report of a

Jemadar, located at Kumpil, by Captain Bradford.'

"I also wrote to the Foreign Secretary with the Governor-General, informing him that certain Oude Chiefs wished to open a communication with me, but that I could do nothing in the matter without the Governor-General's permission.

"*Sunday*, 24*th*. — Sent in the following memorandum to Sir Colin: —

"'Peera Hurkaruh, employed by Mahomed Uskuree and Mahomed Mohsun, left Lucknow on Monday, 18th current (one day later than the last messenger to Hurdeo Bux), and reports as follows:

"'The Begum (mother of the present King of Oude) had just held a Durbar, on which occasion she summoned all the native commandants of troops and the rebel Chiefs, and told them that she was unable to keep them in the pay of the King any longer, and that she desired to pay them up, and discharge them.

"'The soldiers and rebels replied that in a day or two they would attack the British force near Alumbagh, and either drive the British out of the place, or perish in the attempt.

"'A general attack upon General Outram's position is expected.

"'But a letter from Sheikh Fuzl Kureem informs us that the Oude Chukladars and provincial Chiefs, Nazims, &c., hearing of the advance of British troops towards Oude, will make no revenue payments to the nominal King at Lucknow, and that although the Begum and her Minister, Shurfoodowla, have urged the troops to guard the ferries, and to press the Nazims for payment, they (the soldiers) refuse to leave Lucknow; so he argues it is very doubtful whether they will keep their promise of attacking the British force.

"'Nana Sahib is absent from his camp; has left his tents with about one hundred men, at Mulaon; is either in his Zenana at Biroa, or gone to Rhyrabad.

"'The Chukladar of Tundyaon with Dul Singh and other Talookdars, seven thousand men and six guns, is moving towards Newra Ghat on the Ganges. (This is nearly opposite Kanouj.)'

"*Monday*, 25*th*.— Rode to the city; I spoke to the Commander-in-Chief about the Kaemgunge rebels, and gave him the following note on the subject:—

"'From several reports from Kumpil and Shumsabad, I gather that a considerable rebel force of cavalry and zemindarry levies of matchlock men, with several guns, some say nine, some say twelve, are moving towards Furuckabad, and intend to halt to-day at Bunourie, which is three coss from the Mhow gate of the city.

"'They give out that they intend to attack the city, &c. &c., and to fight.

"'They are doubtless encouraged by the bad characters in the city, whom it has not been easy for the Magistrate to identify or to expel hitherto.

"'These men might get over the city wall, and

plunder and do mischief, and the Magistrate has no sufficient force as yet to prevent them.'

"*Tuesday*, 26*th.*—Rode to the city, saw in the Kotwallie (police station) the bodies of two of the Nawabs who had been implicated in the murders and robberies of our poor countrymen at Futteygurh. They had just been hanged by order of the Magistrate. I rode over to see their houses, and notwithstanding my indignation at the conduct of the Nawabs of Furuckabad, the sight was a sad one. A fine palace full of every luxurious appliance, mirrors, chandeliers, lustres, pictures, books, and furniture, suddenly deserted—not a human creature left—save one or two withered hags, in the Zenana; cats, parrots, pet dogs, clamorous for food. Outside, in the shady terraces and summer houses, and round the family mausoleum, wandered animals in quest of water or food, nylghai*, barasingha (twelve-horned deer), and other pet deer; on the wall a little black puppy yelping, and a dog howling piteously; in the poultry yard geese shut up, and making a frightful noise; at the stables grain for seven horses ready steeped and in separate portions, but the horses pawing, looking round, and starving, with food in their sight; monkeys, cockatoos, and an elephant, who had broken loose, and was helping himself to food—formed one of the strangest yet saddest pictures I ever saw. I took care that the animals were fed. As for the princes who so lately were masters of all this luxury, nobody had ventured even to claim their bodies,

* Blue-deer.

and it remained for strangers to give them decent sepulture.

"It seems but the other day that I, then Magistrate of Furuckabad, breakfasted in this very garden house with some of the family who, though receiving princely fortunes at our hands, have now been so ready to slay and spoil their benefactors! How odious is every scene here, once so pleasing to me.

"As I know that the rebels are coming down upon us, I have been round the city outside, from the Mhow Gate. The walls are good for nothing, and it is useless trying to repair them.

"On my return home, I was reading my letters, when Sir Colin came up to my tent, and told me the details of the force which Sir John Lawrence was sending down to Umballa to operate on Rohilcund. He then went on to the next tent to call upon Sir A. Wilson, who has just joined the Camp to command the Artillery.

"At noon General Mansfield called, and told me that a brigade would march at ten this evening to disperse the rascals at Shumshabad, &c. In the afternoon General Grant and Hodson called. The latter remarked to me that his Sikhs are anxiously watching our treatment of mutineers. They say, 'Just now you are very angry with the Sepoys, but six months hence the Lord Sahib (Governor-General) will pardon them all.' Hodson is clearly of opinion, that unless the mutineers are fairly hunted down and sentenced either to death or transportation for life, that we may expect before long a Sikh mutiny. They are watching to see whether mutiny is not condoned by the British Government, and if it is condoned the Sikhs will have their turn; for they will argue, 'If we get the best of it we gain every thing, and if we lose we shall be as well off as we were before.' These are the natural speculations of semi-barbarous men.

"At night I warned Mr. Power* for duty, to go out with the brigade. I found it difficult to convince him that two thousand men, quietly slumbering around, would in the course of half-an-hour be under arms, and on the march to attack the enemy. Scarce a creature in the camp, save General Mansfield, Brigadier Adrian Hope, Hodson and I, knew the plans of the Commander-in-Chief. The men had gone to bed as usual, when quietly orders were issued, and by half-past ten Adrian Hope, with his brigade †, was on his march through Furuckabad to attack the enemy, who were encamped some twelve miles from the city near Shumshabad.

"*Wednesday*, 27*th*.—Golab Rai Duffadar, of Hodson's Horse, arrived at my tent this evening. He states, thus: 'On arriving at Roshunabad at daybreak, Captain Hodson ascertained that the enemy were encamped in force at Shumshabad. A body of their cavalry, about four hundred in number, were

* Mr. John Power was Magistrate of Furuckabad. It was he who so gallantly held Mynpoorie with Major Raikes, throughout June 1857, in spite of the mutiny and desertion of the Sepoys there stationed.

† Two squadrons 9th Lancers, 200 Hodson's Horse, one troop and one battery Bengal Artillery, 43rd Royal Highlanders, 53rd Regiment, 4th Punjab Rifles.

preparing to charge our cavalry. Hodson went at them with his Horse; they ran, leaving four guns. Hodson pursued for two miles; twenty-five or thirty of the enemy stood, fought, and were cut to pieces. Our artillery blew up one of the enemy's ammunition waggons. I saw five or six of Hodson's Horse *hors de combat.* I saw no European private soldiers killed. Captain McDouall* is badly wounded. Hodson has two sword cuts in his arm. I saw hundreds of the enemy dead on the field.'

"So much for Golab Rai's story.—He had a cut on his thumb, and asked for a little brandy. I asked how much; half a bottle was the reply. He took this down almost at one gulp. As he had been in the saddle about twenty-four hours, and fighting into the bargain, it will do him no harm. I sent him to my Sikh escort to get his supper, and took his news, a letter from Mr. Power, and the following original production from my Moonshee, over to Sir Colin's mess tent.

"'SIR,

"'We have just returned from the field of battle and pitched our tents, but we have not taken any thing yet, but Mr. Power has ordered to bring *rusud* (supplies) very soon.

"'The action was commenced at eight o'clock. We found the rebels at Sootia, half a mile in the direction of Mhow from Shumshabad; after having

* This excellent officer, who was Captain Hodson's second in command, and right-hand man, sunk under his wound, to the sorrow of all who knew his rare value as a soldier.

fired a few balls they ran away: Captain Hodson's cavalry pursued them for more than two miles, and killed numbers of the rebels. A great many were shot by our guns, two were found hidden in a cave, seven in kurbee (high tall cultivation); they were shot, and two caught who are still alive in our Camp. One of them is a boy of twelve years of age. He says he came to watch his fields, the rebels forcibly took him in their Camp. The other is a man of (full) age. Great number of the enemy was killed. — The loss on our side is nothing, but Captains Hodson and Steel have been wounded, and one European killed. — Five or six native soldiers were killed. — The rebels have run away in the direction of Soonijpoor Ghat. The enemy will find no shelter anywhere, the villagers have been highly oppressed by them, and have refused admittance in their village.

" 'Captain Mc Douall's one leg has been shot off. Captain Hodson has been wounded in his right hand in two places, but not severely. We have taken four guns of first rate from the enemy.

" 'This is first time I have seen a battle; first when I saw ball passing by me I was highly frightened and moved little back, but Mr. Power moved forward, then I followed him, and remained the whole time with Mr. Power.

" 'Our camp is to day at Sootia, which was in the morning in the possession of our enemies.

" 'We are very glad in succeeding in routing totally the enemy; the names of the chiefs are Mooltan Khan and Neaz Ahmud, the former is the inhabitant of Mhow, the latter of Bareilly; the men

entirely beaten and broken. Neaz Ahmud Khan was wounded in two places, and his nephew was killed. To the best of my calculation, the Bareilly army numbered from eight to ten thousand, and the English two thousand fighting men. When roll was called on this side at Ooseyt, twelve hundred men were missing."

The papers* taken in the field by Mr. Power enabled me to lay before Sir Colin a pretty accurate statement of the resources of the enemy. They were full of complaints that the Hindoos along the left bank of the Ganges were in league with the English.

"*Saturday*, 30*th*.—In order to protect the river Ghats, I determined to call out yeomanry levies, as it was impossible to get soldiers, or good policemen. I accordingly summoned some of the bravest Rajpoot clans, who, during the last six months

* Amongst other quaint documents was the following charm, taken from the dead body of the General's nephew, which was left on the battle-field.

1	14	11	8
12	7	2	13
6	9	16	3
15	4	5	10

Thirty-four, count it as you like.

had been ón their own account, and in self-defence, at war with the rebel Nawab of Furuckabad.

"These men, on the promise of good pay, were only too happy to watch Sheorajpore Ghat, Mhow, Shumshabad, Rajpore, &c. &c. I had four hundred of them posted at once.*

"They have their own arms, and vow they will not allow a rebel to cross the river. They understand that their services are merely required *pro tempore*, and the arrangement suits them. The head man is to have 100 rupees per mensem as Thanadar (chief of police), his Jemadars (or sergeants) are to have 20 rupees, privates 7 rupees. Thus, these unruly spirits and strong hands are enlisted on our side, and we shall have not only their sympathy, as before, but also their aid for the future.

"I forwarded the following information, which I obtained through Mr. Capper †, to Sir Colin.

"'THE BILGRAM HURKARUH.

"'Left Lucknow on the 22nd.

"'Shekh Dost Ally, commandant, still hankering after Menra and Jussomalnow; the Tehseeldar pressing for revenue; the people refusing.

"'A large force still at Lucknow, but disorgan-

* Up to the time I left India, these men had done excellent service, and effectually guarded the river, &c.

† Mr. Capper was a Deputy Commissioner in Oude before the mutiny, and was noticed, for his gallant conduct during the siege of Lucknow (into which place he with difficulty escaped), by General Inglis. His ability and local knowledge were of great value to us all.

ised; no man will go out to fight a second time; the only combatants being the mutineers, who are now desperate.

"'These mutineers have chief authority in Lucknow, and have forbidden 'making beef';* they have well fortified the Begum's Palace in the Kaisarbagh, having built a double timber wall and filled in the interval with mud; many guns are already in position, and they daily cast more; all the *big guns* have been taken into Kaisarbagh, leaving none out. There are certainly about 30,000 Sepoys on duty at the Kaisarbagh.

"'On the 23rd, two Sowars from Bareilly brought in a letter from Khan Bahadoor Khan.

"'The Chukledar publishes that the Punjab army has mutinied, and having already taken Delhi is marching down.

"'Two Nujeeb regiments and some guns (not known how many), have reached Husungunge. Lukhawut Hossein (the faithful Zemindar of Alrowlee) has seen them; Sufdur Alee Risaldar has returned to Bilgram; some say he is waiting for orders from the Nana.

"'There are no guns at the Ghats, and the Sepoys are badly off for powder and lead.

"'The Shahjee about the 23rd attempted to seize the Government at Lucknow; the Queen Mother resisted; and they fired big guns and muskets at each other; the Shahjee was defeated, and a large portion of the city was looted, the

* The killing of cows.

fight having been in the Chouk. It is not known where the Shahjee is.

"'Mohamed Hoseen Khan, who was defeated at Goruckpore, is recruiting at Sanda (near Fyzabad), and at the special request of Man Sing, six regiments of mutineers and a battery have been sent down to him from Lucknow.

"'The following may be relied on:—

"'The Nana's force (now increased to about 2000 men), is at Seetulgunge, (about five and a half koss from Bangurmow), but his own whereabouts is uncertain. He has engaged many men resembling him in face and figure, and is always in disguise. To ask whether he is in the camp is punishable with death.

"'The Nana sent a man to Bareilly on the 27th, and a second to Furuckabad.

"'At Lucknow want of coin is much felt; the nobles are melting down all their plate, and even the religious ornaments are used for pay of troops.

"'January 28th, 1858.'

"Rode to see Hodson, he is much cut up about McDouall's loss, but treats his own wounds very lightly. Being in his sword arm, we shall lose his invaluable services for a time."

Here I take leave of my journal.

It was not my lot to see much more of the stirring scenes passing around. On hearing from Sir Colin that there was a probability of an advance on Oude, without making any further demonstration upon Rohilcund, in the first moments of bitter disappointment, I applied (somewhat impulsively) for the only office which in my opinion (and, I believe, in the opinion of the Commander-in-Chief), could have enabled me with due regard to his service and to my own position, to accompany His Excellency beyond the limits of my own (the North-Western) Provinces. In these provinces my authority was for the time being paramount, but across the river in the Oude territory I had not any jurisdiction whatever. I therefore asked Lord Canning, if it seemed fit, to constitute me Agent to the Governor-General with the Commander-in-Chief. I explained that I was receiving overtures from the Oude people, but that of course I could hold no sort of communication with them without his Lordship's sanction.

Before I received any reply, the Commander-in-Chief made a rapid visit to the Governor-General, at Allahabad, and I, with his permission, brought my family from Meerut to Cawnpore. Here, on the 24th of February, I took leave of Sir Colin Campbell, Lord Canning having, for doubtless very good and sufficient reasons, declined to accede to my proposition to accompany the Commander-in-Chief as Agent to the Governor-General.

Putting aside the state of my health and my private affairs, which rendered my return to England desirable, I bowed to the decision of the Governor-General with deep regret. It was impossible not to feel more than ordinary pain at leaving Sir Colin Campbell. Not only had his courage, skill, and justice, won the unfeigned respect of every officer in the service of the East India Company under his command, but his hearty, frank, and cordial nature at once commanded the affection of those who, like me, had the good fortune to be in unreserved communication with him. To make further remark on a personage who I trust may long be spared to us, were superfluous; to say less, impossible.

I had opportunity enough to watch the workings of a mind in which duty was the sole law. It was a fortunate circumstance, due to the personal characters of both, that so perfect a cordiality existed between the Governor-General and the Commander-in-Chief.* Their views may not have been identical as to the line of policy to be pursued, but whatever Lord Canning thought should be done, that Sir Colin delighted to execute.

I have seen in the public prints animadversions

* Sir Colin gave me the following account of the reported "*misunderstanding*" between him and the Governor-General, which once caused serious public uneasiness, and resulted in explanations in Parliament:—

One sultry evening, not long after Sir Colin's arrival in Calcutta, where he was the guest of Lord and Lady Canning, Sir David Baird reminded him that dinner was just coming on the table. Sir Colin had been writing despatches all day, was too tired to make a regular dinner toilette, and, taking Sir David by the arm, strolled across to a neighbouring hotel, where they took a quiet chop and bottle of claret.

The next day it was all over Calcutta that Sir Colin had so serious a misunderstanding with Lord Canning that he had actually left Government House.

on the conduct of civilians who are said to have interfered with the Commander-in-Chief. I can only say, that no civilian in a state of mental sanity would for one moment have ventured to make any suggestion to Sir Colin, other than a mere recital of facts which it was necessary for the Chief to know. But if it is meant that the Supreme Civil Power dictated measures of imperial policy to the head of the army, then I can only say, that Sir Colin was the first man to accept the duties of a soldier, and the very last to question the authority of the State.

It is not for me to discuss what may have been Sir Colin Campbell's views regarding the move upon Rohilcund or upon Lucknow in January last,—that was a matter between His Excellency and the Governor-General in Council. But I may briefly state my own opinions.

I had every personal reason to desire earnestly the advance on Rohilcund. This would have kept me with Sir Colin, and in a position as Civil Dictator, which any man might covet. If this advance had been made at once, soon after Sir Colin's arrival at Futteygurh, the consequences would have been important, so far that our Government would have been then restored without any formidable opposition in Rohilcund.

But the operations against Lucknow would have been delayed, and the rebel or mutineer force in Lucknow much strengthened by the accession of the Rohillas. If, then, Sir Colin could have disposed of the Rohilcund affair, as I think he desired, and as perhaps he might, in all January and February, there would still have been time to go at Lucknow. But there was no certainty that Rohilcund could be so soon disposed of, and for reasons of imperial policy it was absolutely necessary that Lucknow should at latest be attacked in March ; therefore, on the whole, however much opposed to my private interests, I must allow that the policy pursued has been as sound as it has also proved successful.

I had frequent conversations with Sir Colin as to the issue of a proclamation on his advance into Oude. His expression was, that he desired a public proclamation to form his advanced guard on his re-entering Oude. We always believed that any such notification from the Supreme Government would simply announce to the people that the irresistible British army had come to punish all mutineers, rebels, and traitors, but not to carry war to the homes of the people.

In alluding to this proclamation, in conversation with Lord Canning, I understood from his Lordship that the only difference of opinion between himself and the Commander-in-Chief was whether the proclamation should precede, as Sir Colin proposed, or as the Governor-General preferred, follow immediately the actual re-occupation of Lucknow.

Without offering an opinion on the notification which has caused so much discussion in England, I would remark, that in time of war the people of India care very little what is proclaimed; they look to acts, not to words. If we can beat our enemies in the field the people will accept our policy* without further question. What that policy should be I now proceed to discuss.

I gladly bring the personal part of my narrative to a close; indeed I should not have considered these passages worthy of the public eye, but for the support which they may give to the opinions which I am about to offer to the consideration of my countrymen.

* To speak technically as a revenue officer, the real blot in the proclamation, one entirely overlooked in the parliamentary discussion, was not so much the threatened confiscation of the landed property of rebellious Talookdars, as the cession of full rights in their holdings to certain men named in the notification. The Governor-General had no legal authority to guarantee rights or privileges to these persons without specific reservation of the allodial rights of the subordinate occupiers of the soil.

CHAP. XI.

THE RECONSTITUTION OF THE POLICE AND NATIVE ARMY IN THE NORTH-WESTERN PROVINCES.

EARLY in September, whilst we were still nearly confined to within the walls of the Agra Fort, the Lieutenant-Governor desired me to draw up a scheme for restoring the Police of the North-Western Provinces.

I submitted a rough note, which formed the outline of a more complete Report elaborated by Major Williams, Superintendent of Police. The whole plan thus improved was, as I understand, sanctioned by Lord Canning before I left India. I quote here the memorandum submitted to Mr. Colvin on the 5th September, 1857 *: —

"The late disturbances have been caused :

"First. By a general mutiny of the Native Army.

"Secondly. By the violence and rapacity of the Goojur, Mewattie, and other clans, disposed in the best times to predatory habits; also by the cruelty of the lower town-mobs and cantonment rabble.

"Lastly. By the attempts of certain quasi-royal

* Slightly enlarged.

pensioners and landholders to revive their lost local ascendency.

"We can hardly expect the Police to come up to the mark of regular soldiers, but if organised, with some important modifications, in the manner of the Punjab Police, a very efficient body might be raised, capable of putting down all local disturbances, and of making the internal Civil Government generally independent of the regular Army.

"In these provinces, the public peace has been preserved, treasuries guarded, and despatches of treasure from one station to another escorted by the Sepoys of the Bengal Native Infantry.

"In order to dispense entirely and for ever with these guards, who have not only failed us in the hour of need, but have themselves placed our empire in jeopardy, I propose that an 'organised Police Force, Horse and Foot,' should be at once raised. Of the material I shall speak presently, merely premising that it should differ from the late Bengal Army *in toto*.

"For each district something like one hundred horse and four hundred foot organised Policemen should be enlisted.

"The horsemen should receive not less than 20 rupees and not more than 25 rupees per mensem, finding their own horses, and generally armed and equipped on the model of the Punjab Police, as organised under Sir Henry Lawrence, Sir John Lawrence, General Chamberlain, and other competent authorities.

"The foot Policemen should receive the rate of pay lately enjoyed by the Bengal Sepoy.

"We should thus have under the Commissioner of each division a force of about five hundred horse and two thousand foot organised Policemen, commanded by a Captain or a Major of the line, who would ordinarily be quartered at the Commissioner's Station, the head-quarters of the Division, and who would superintend the entire divisional organised Police Force.

"A Lieutenant of the line should drill and dress the detachments of these men posted at the Sudder or chief station of each district. His head-quarters should ordinarily be with the Magistrate, to whom he should be attached as an assistant or joint-magistrate. This Lieutenant, with the concurrence of the Magistrate, should have power, on proceedings duly held and recorded, to dismiss any private Policeman, without appeal. *No Court-martial should be allowed.* In like manner, the Commissioner and divisional Commandant should have power to dismiss any native non-commissioned officer. Native commissioned officers (who should, as far as possible, be native gentlemen of family) should only be liable to dismissal by the orders of the local Government.

"The location and disposition of the police force would rest with the Magistrate, subject to the orders of the Commissioner.

"Tour of duty of the same detachment of police, never to exceed three years in any one district.

"*Material.*

"It is far easier to propose a fitting organisation for a police force, than to decide upon the material of which such a body should consist. The native police of the North Western Provinces have proved unfaithful to their salt, when opposed to mutinous soldiers of their own country, and the higher the organisation of such police, the readier have they been to set up as mutineers, and hurry to join the revolted Sepoys at Delhi.* The organised police in Oude have behaved as badly as the regulars, and if we had been unfortunate enough on this side of the Ganges to have entertained any such force, our dangers and difficulties would have been so far increased.

"We have learned now from bitter experience, that in India, as elsewhere, the people of the country can only be kept in subjection by strangers through the instrumentality of a *foreign* army. We can no more hold these provinces by native troops, without a preponderating power of English or other foreign soldiers, than Austria could hold Italy by Italians, or France hold Africa by African soldiers alone.

"For police purposes we cannot be supplied with European soldiers, so we must look for the next best material at hand.

"Without going into too minute ethnological

* The jail guards, who were drilled and dressed in uniform, were the first to turn against their employers.

details, I may just observe that for such a province as Rohilcund, where the Mahomedans have proved treacherous, and for some time to come may prove turbulent, we should use regiments of organised Police embodied on the plan of the Punjab Guides, but with a strong dash of Hindoo or quasi Hindoo tribes, such as Dogras, Sikhs, Muzubees, Goorkhas and Keechees.

"For the Benares Province where there is a dense Hindoo population, there might be a stronger infusion of Afghans, Beloochees, or Punjab Mahomedans. Such men as form the Puthan element in Coke's Punjab Guides, would sympathise as little with the people, and put down an émeute in Benares, as easily as a dragoon from Hounslow or Aldershot, and with much less expense to the State. It may be possible to get mounted riflemen from the Cape, and stout Africans from Sierra Leone, or the Gambia River, as employed in our West India regiments, and I need not point out that the vigour of the former, and docility and strength of the latter, would make them invaluable soldiers in India, though better suited for the regular army than the Police. Lastly, a proportion of Rajpoots from Rohilcund, Aheers from Mynpoorie, Jats from Allygurh, and other tribes who have behaved so admirably during our late troubles, might well be amalgamated with the alien masses already described."

So much for the organised Police, and now to turn to the Rural Constabulary Force:—

"In the higher divisions, *i.e.* nearest the Punjab,

I would absorb the old Khalsa Sikhs as far as they will go, thus conferring a benefit on the Punjab and North-Western Provinces alike. The rest should be of the Hindostanee portion of the material above indicated.

"The military officers in charge of the organised Police should be required to keep one-fifth part of the Rural Constabulary Force under drill, at District head-quarters.

"They should be taught to use the old flint and steel fire-locks, and undergo a modicum of drill, just enough to teach them to move together, load, fire, and march in order."

I was to have discussed this scheme with the Lieutenant-Governor on the 7th of September last, but he was too ill to see me, and on the 9th he died.

At a subsequent period I notified to Government my cordial approbation of a system of yeomanry levies, which I think was first proposed by that accomplished officer, Mr. Edward Anderdon Reade, senior member of the Revenue Board at Agra. On this subject some information will be found in Chapter X., where I have described the practical use I made of yeomanry levies when Civil Commissioner with Sir Colin Campbell.

The scheme thus hastily sketched would give for the North-Western Provinces, exclusive of the Delhi Division (which has been made over to the Punjab), the following force:—

27 Districts, each 100 Horse - 2,700 Police Sowars.
Do. Do. 400 Foot - 10,800 Police Foot.

I have put down twenty-seven districts, because the district of Goruckpore, with a population of three millions, *must* be divided into two Zillahs.

This force will keep the public peace in our North-Western Provinces easily when once order has been restored, and will furnish guards for all public offices, treasuries, jails, convoys, &c.

The regular army, relieved of these duties, may safely be reduced in proportion.

Thus far I have dealt with a question familiar to my mind. In proceeding to offer a few suggestions on matters of a more purely military nature, I ask indulgence.

The military force which should, in my opinion, suffice to hold the North-Western Provinces in their present state, with the aid of an organised Police Corps, I set down thus:—

Civil Division.	Cavalry.	Infantry.
Meerut	2000	4000
Rohilcund	2000	4000
Agra	1500	4000
Allahabad	1500	4000
Benares	1500	4000
Grand total	8500	20,000

With an organised Police Force two-thirds of the military would be available for service in any direction. But for service beyond the Peninsula of India it would be prudent to employ Asiatics, in other words, to take away as few Europeans as possible.

The proportion of military and organised Police Force to the population should be gradually reduced in the North-Western Provinces from the standard here given to about one thousand foot, and two hundred and fifty horse, for each million. Thus, the proposed regular army of horse and foot for the North-Western Provinces might be gradually lowered to eighteen thousand foot, and four thousand five hundred horse, leaving the organised Police at the full numbers originally proposed.

The proportion of Europeans to native soldiers need not exceed one-fourth of the regular military force. Thus, for the provinces under notice, we should require eventually only four thousand five hundred British infantry and about eleven hundred cavalry.

This proportion might be reduced by the employment of Africans, such men as are now enlisted for service in our West India regiments, who would stand the climate well, and are celebrated for docility, physical strength, and temperate habits. And of the European portion of the force one-fourth might be Germans, Italians, or Swiss mercenaries, so far as Indian considerations are concerned.

I leave it for more experienced hands to fix the number of artillerymen required. The force must be a powerful one. When right is on our side, as I trust for the future it will be in India, there is no such diplomatist as your twenty-four pounder. Whatever the artillery force may be, one precaution seems indispensable. All and every sort of great gun should be kept in the hands of Europeans, and Europeans alone. The natives of India should have nothing to do with the preparation, manipulation, or custody of our ordnance stores. Strict precautions on this head, such as were originally * introduced by the Court of Directors (so far as the natives are concerned), would at once infinitely increase our power and lessen our danger in India. Guns are to the natives what ships are to Great Britain. The possessor of the strongest artillery is the master of India; and although we can generally take their guns, and the natives seldom indeed have managed to deprive us of our artillery in open fight, yet, to restore our prestige and to maintain it, we must be clearly masters in this respect.

For laboratory duties Africans would be available, and should at once be employed.

On the number of guns and artillerymen kept up by native independent Powers, we should keep a jealous eye; and in independent States we should positively restrict, if possible, the accumulation of cannon, sulphur, shot, or shell.

To enable the Magistrate to do his duty, the inhabitants of our own territories should be disarmed, and an Act similar to the Punjab Arms Act sternly enforced.

The future constitution of our native regiments in Bengal and the Punjab is an anxious and difficult question.

* Bengal Artillery: Calcutta Review, No. 18, June, 1848.

Lately at Delhi all eyes were on "the Guides," who, mounted on camels and dromedaries, came hurrying down to mix in the struggle. The Punjab regiments looked up to the Guides as their model: had they faltered the consequences would have been serious indeed. But, when the Guides, under their admirable officers, plunged boldly into the thickest of the fight, shedding their blood like water for the nation who had so lately deprived them of their national liberty, every Englishman from Peshawur to Calcutta breathed more freely. We saw at once that the Sikhs were on our side; what the Guides had done, other Punjabee regiments would attempt. The prophecy which Mr. Colvin had made to me in May was to be fulfilled, "John Lawrence and the Sikhs will re-conquer Hindostan."

Now the secret of the success of our Guide Corps, and of some other Punjab regiments made on the same model, and inspired, as I believe, by the genius of Sir Henry Lawrence, is simply this:—

As a rule, each company, or troop, consists of a separate nationality, or of men of one country and native officers of another. Take for example the following analysis of the Punjab Guide Infantry, at a late period:

No. 1. Company comprised all sorts of up-countrymen, *i. e.* high up in or above the Punjab, under down-country (Poorubeea) native officers. This was familiarly called the Roolla Moolla (olla podrida) company.

No. 2. Puthans from Peshawur, fierce, relentless, and savage-looking.

No. 3. Punjabee Mahomedans from Lahore or Sealkote, from the banks of the Beas, the Ravee, and the Chenab. Tall, sleek, good-natured, quiet men, easily managed in the lines, and ready to cut off the head of a brother Mahomedan in Hindostan when duty required.

No. 4. Khas (pure) Afreedees, speaking Pushtoo.

No. 5. Goorkhas from Nepal, brave little fellows, with high cheek bones, eagle eyes, fond of cricket, shooting, fishing, and fighting.

No. 6. Sikhs, tall, wiry, long-enduring, from the Manjha or mid-country, between the Beas and Ravee.

The Cavalry Guide Corps was composed on the same principle.

In regiments thus constituted there is a perpetual rivalry of company against company, or troop against troop. National as well as regimental jealousies and antipathies prevent combination. Thus we come back to the old lesson, "*Divide and Conquer.*" Had our Bengal army been constituted on this plan no weapon formed against us could have prospered.

In reconstituting our native army, and to some extent in forming an organised Police Force, we must take the Punjab Guide Corps as our model, if we would never drift into mutiny again.

It will not do to adopt the easier and more obvious plan of throwing separate nationalities into distinct bodies. We do not want Indian regiments cemented together by the bond of a common country or faith, but we want regiments composed of various elements, incapable of cohesion or absorption, yet under the strong hand of the European fit for powerful and united action. It is this mixture of unity, as a whole, with diversity in the component parts, which gives the perfect organisation. Such a body is safe to the State, and terrible to the enemies of the State alone.

Separate regiments may revolt and do mischief any day, but a separate troop or company can hardly rise in mutiny, because the other troops or companies would at once combine to cut off the offender.

But as it will be found practically impossible to carry this mode of organisation out in every case, we must, as the only safe alternative, grasp still at the principle here set forth. If we cannot have enough mixed regiments, then to make up the deficiency, the Punjab must garrison Hindostan, Hindostan the Punjab.

The latest researches of our best antiquarians show that the old Romans employed the levies from one province to hold the garrison of another. We must to some extent do the same. A Sikh will not mutiny at Benares, to run the gauntlet thence to Lahore amidst a nation of enemies. Neither will the men of Hindostan try a second time the experiment of running from Lahore to Benares.

A few words in conclusion on the character of the British officer who is to lead these regiments, and who, instead of being thwarted by a system of centralisation, should have full power over his men. Sir Henry Lawrence's system being the best for our purpose in forming a regiment, we may take Sir Henry also as our model of a regimental commander. The Friends of M. Guizot called him "*un rosier en fer*;" this is just the description of what Sir Henry was, of what his bosom friends, Lake, Reynell Tayler, and Robert Napier still are. Men of this stamp have a marvellous power over rough natures; but whether we have the "*rosier*" or not, the "*fer*" is absolutely indispensable in a leader of Sikhs or Afreedees. The almost superhuman power of Nicholson over the Sikhs was to be found in a perfectly just, yet relentlessly firm temper, and a bold and noble presence. "The tramp of his war-horse might be heard two miles off." Such was the description given of Nicholson by a rough Sikh who wept over his grave. A mere easy, good-natured man, who can only be *nurum* (soft), and never *gurrum* (hot), will not do for the Sikhs. The mixture of quiet benevolence and justice, with an ardent spirit, chains them to a leader for ever.

CHAP. XII.

RELIGION AND EDUCATION.

I PROCEED now shortly to consider the duties of the British Government with regard to religion and education in India.

The mysteries of the native mind have been so far disclosed during the revolt, that it seems less difficult by the light thus given to discuss the great and kindred questions of religion and education. If one fact was, during the late troubles, more clearly demonstrated than another, it was this, that the body of the natives hated our system of village schools, whilst they clung to our colleges. The reasons for this preference and aversion appear to be these: The village schools were generally supported by a subscription of one per cent. on the Government revenue. The influence of local officers was enough to induce the landholders to grant this cess, but at heart the ignorant Zemindars looked upon the whole scheme with suspicion and aversion, as calculated to interfere with their religion and their pocket at the same time.

On the other hand, the payments to the colleges were purely voluntary; and the education given in the English language, and in the missionary colleges in the Christian doctrine, had the effect of enlisting the affections of the students. The boy, who had been instructed in the morality of the Gospel, and had tasted the literature of the West, grew up as a man into the admirer and often the partisan of the English. During the course of the mutiny, numerous English scholars who had offices under our Government came in to us at Agra, from Oude, Rohilcund, and the Doab. All evinced a spirit of determined loyalty to their British employers, and many suffered death merely as English scholars, at the hands of the mutineers. A Bengalee Baboo* at Furuckabad or Cawnpore, was almost in as great peril as a Christian, so long as those cities were in the hands of the rebels. Not that the Baboo had personally any taste for the honours of martyrdom; for to tell the truth, he was the veriest coward under the sun, but simply because the Sepoy instinctively hated the English scholars, as part and parcel of the English community. But the students of Agra, Furuckabad, Benares, Delhi, or Bareilly, who had been instructed either at the Government or Mission Colleges, behaved in a much bolder manner, and often at the risk of their own lives openly declared their adherence to the British cause.

It is further to be remarked, that it is education in and by the English language, and that alone, which has seemed to chain the student to our fortunes. Some of our bitterest enemies were the

* These men are generally employed as English writers in Upper India.

native doctors and surgeons who had studied European science in the vernacular all their lives.

I here introduce a letter written to me on this subject by the Reverend Principal of the Agra Church Missionary College. It will have weight with those who know, as I do, how entirely free Mr. French is from any bias of mind or professional prejudice:—

"From what Dr. Anderson* tells me of the youths of the Delhi College, and from what I have observed personally of the conduct of my boys in Agra, I have no hesitation in stating it as my conviction, that the result of an English—more particularly of a Christian English education—is to bind to us the hearts of the youth of this country by a link stronger than any other which has been yet discovered.

"The boys' good feeling and well wishing towards the English Government seems to have been almost precisely proportionate to the length of time they had been under our training and the extent to which they had imbibed our religious, moral, and scientific teaching. It was not merely that they professed a hollow attachment to our interests when they saw which way things were likely to turn; but throughout they showed themselves capable of taking an honest and independent part in the support of those principles of order and just government with which their education had led them to sympathise. When among them, I quite

* Professor of Moral Philosophy at the Government Colleges.

lost the sense of being with those whose interests and whose wishes lay in a different direction from my own."

To the testimony of Mr. French I wish to add my own ; not only in support of what he has here advanced—which, from my own observation, I know to be correct,—but also from the wide acquaintance which I had with native civil officers all over Upper India. I found it to be a general rule, that where you had an official well educated at our English colleges, and conversant with the English tongue, there you had a friend upon whom reliance could be placed. So few were the English scholars amongst our enemies, that it was the custom of the mutineers to burn our intercepted despatches rather than attempt to get them deciphered. They would trust nobody who even knew English. I may be reminded that Nana Sahib's Minister was an English scholar ; but the exceptions are sufficiently rare to prove the rule.

Such then was the conduct of the men whose chief tie to us was an English education. The little body of native converts who had openly professed Christianity identified themselves entirely with their co-religionists, and evinced their sincerity by accepting all the difficulties of our position and throwing their lot heartily in with our own. Their cause and the Englishman's cause was one, and many of them sealed the confession of their faith with their blood.

I conclude, therefore, that this is not the time to press vernacular education on the people. But, the Government should fix a standard of secular education, *including English Literature as a sine quâ non*, and bestow a liberal grant in aid to all schools coming up to that standard.

Further than this, there has been the best encouragement to restore* or keep up, as the case may be, the Government Colleges in which English has hitherto been taught, and every boy at these seminaries should be put through a course of English, *pari passu* with any other branch of education. The village schools may in the North-Western Provinces be left to themselves until the people see the need, and seek for the appliances of a higher course of study.

To turn to the subject of Religion. The worst enemies to Christianity in India have been Christians. So far then it is the duty of Government to provide suitable pastors for the great religious divisions of their servants, that neither Episcopalian, Presbyterian, nor Roman Catholic should by his brutality or ignorance bring discredit upon the profession of Christianity.

Every Indian village has its temple or mosque, and it was a disgrace, happily now forgotten, that for years the soldiers of our armies met to worship

* Wherever Mission premises, libraries, or Churches have been destroyed by the people, at the instigation of the mutineers, it is incumbent on the Government to levy the amount from the district. Sir John Lawrence and Mr. Montgomery did thus at Lodiana, where the people helped the mutineers in doing mischief. They were fined the full amount of damage done, and the money paid over to the Mission.

God in the barrack or the riding school. The Government, especially in the Punjab, have now liberally helped their servants to build Churches and Chapels, and this reproach no longer exists. Let the Hindoo and Mahomedan see clearly that whilst we boldly profess our own, we desire not to constrain their mode of belief; that though we are not indifferent to all religions, we treat all men alike. If we hold India as conquerors, we rule it as moderators. Our vocation is to keep the public peace, not to govern the public mind. If a Hindoo thinks proper to paint his nose with vermilion, to tie his hair in knots, to squander his money on nautch girls, or pagodas, let him do so. But when he wants to sacrifice his infant children to the river gods, to sing filthy songs on the highway, or to stop up his grandfather's mouth with mud and then launch him still living into the sacred stream*, our laws should interfere. In like manner, if the Mahomedan solace his spirit by beating his breast, and calling on his prophet or martyrs in public procession, we should allow the procession to pass on; but when he rushes about sword in hand frantic with drugs and fanaticism, we should take away his arms and put him to cool in the nearest police station. Even so, if under the garb of religion, a minister of Christianity were to offend decency, public or private, the law would strip his gown from the offender.

* These so-called "Ghat-murders" go on daily close to Calcutta, and should be put down whether the Bengalee like it or not.

This is the proper display of the grandeur of Christianity. Let the Mahometan, with the Koran on his breast, and the sword in his hand, slay or circumcise; let the Hindoo coolly excommunicate mankind. It is the privilege of the Christian ruler neither to repel nor to force the human family,—to maintain at the same moment public decency and private opinion.

To turn to the duties of public servants in India.

The public servant of Government, whether military or civil, should not attempt to preach a crusade, or spend his time in exhibiting religious dogmas, or discussing doctrinal points with the natives his subordinates, for this reason above all others, that this is the surest way to make hypocrites, not converts. Let the soldier or civilian assist the missionary with his purse, his counsel, or his prayers, but let him not usurp an office which is inconsistent with his obligations to the State.

Such is the duty of the servants of the British Government in India. The responsibilities of England are far more wide. Every missionary sent to the banks of the Ganges is not only a herald of truth, but also of good government.

So far as the Christian teacher rightly educates the heathen mind, he not only fulfils the great commands of his Divine Master, but also incidentally aids and supports the British rule.

The interests of Christian missions and good government are identical, not antagonistic. In supporting and enlarging missions to the heathen of India, we not only offer to the Almighty our humble and dutiful tribute, but also to the best of our means contribute to the happiness and well-being of the vast country committed to our care.

CHAP. XIII.

A FEW WORDS ABOUT HOSPITALS IN INDIA.

NOTHING astonished the earliest European traveller in India so much as the solicitude of the Gentoos for insect life, and their profound indifference to human suffering. Men died by the road-side uncared for, but for bugs and fleas regular hospitals were provided. Without waiting to inquire how far this is the natural result of that peculiar apathy of the Asiatic mind which, abhorring active interference with other men, is not in itself averse to the emotions of pity and benevolence, I pass on to consider what is the duty of the British Government with regard to the sick and afflicted amongst the native population.

The character of the physician is highly esteemed in the East. Every schoolboy knows that it was to an expert English doctor we owed our first step towards independence in Bengal, and every Englishman is looked upon as a "*hukeem*," and invited to prescribe for all sorts of ailments in all sorts of impossible conjunctures.

The people then being ready to receive our aid, we should not be backward in giving it, and indeed of late years great efforts have been made to institute dispensaries and hospitals at every large station in the North-Western Provinces and the Punjab.

My own experience leads me to suggest that natives are not fitted *morally* to control these institutions, and I strongly urge that as far as possible the actual local superintendence of the Government dispensaries be henceforth intrusted to European hands alone. If medical education is too expensive in England or Scotland to enable us to import regular practitioners for this work, we should look to Germany for men who at a moderate rate of payment would undertake the duties. The details of such a scheme could easily be elaborated; a medical examiner at Dresden or Vienna might be authorised to pass qualified men into the service, who would find their way viâ Trieste to Calcutta as fast as their services might be required.

These remarks may seem out of place here, but I have seen the hearts of the people so widely interested by a good European doctor, and so thoroughly alienated by a bad Mahomedan or Bengalee practitioner, that I consider it a waste of money, influence, and human life, to go on educating natives of India for high and independent medical charge. The difference between a hukeem or doctor, and a hākim or ruler, is not so great in the native mind, that we can afford to have men like Vuzeer Khan* at Agra, raising the

* Chief native surgeon at the Thomason Hospital College.

green flag of rebellion, and Bose* in the Punjab, offending the people by extortion and cruelty. A wider scrutiny would only confirm my position, that if we wished to strengthen our hold on the native affection, it is expedient and proper to employ European rather than native surgeons, to hold charge of Government hospital institutions.

Working on the basis here proposed, namely, European personal superintendence at the Government dispensaries, it would be easy to combine a leper house, a blind asylum, and a poor house, under the same charge, at every civil station in India.

The lepers should be looked after, not only on their own account, but to prevent them banding themselves into gangs, and under the garb of mendicancy, levying contributions on the public. If the Magistrate prevent, as he is bound to do, this disgusting species of extortion, it is only right that he should be able to point to an asylum where (as at Amritsur and some other places) the leper can be comfortably housed, fed, and cared for.

Lastly, with an European functionary in sole and immediate charge of the charitable institutions at each station, the sick and infirm, who too often

* Bose was imprisoned for appropriating the fixed allowance for medicine and diet at the dispensary of Buttala in the Lahore Division. The sum he thus fraudulently took was about two pounds per mensem; his salary being some four hundred pounds per annum. This man had been educated in England, and had the highest testimonials for skill. The late Governor-General dismissed him from the service.

perish miserably by the way-side, might be cared for. This duty can hardly be confided to a native. I may be reminded that the Civil Surgeon does perform all the duties here indicated at our larger stations. This is true, but I desire to advocate the following modification of existing arrangements:—We have now a Civil Surgeon at large stations, with an extra assistant (native) surgeon under him. Instead of a native, I would introduce an European to the immediate personal and local charge of the dispensaries, and other charitable institutions, who should be subordinate to the Civil Surgeon.

At small stations, where we have now native extra assistant surgeons, I would have Europeans of the same grade. This would be a great boon, both to the civil officers and to the people. The present race of extra assistant native surgeons too often bring the very liberality of our Government into disrepute.

CHAP XIV.

THE BENGAL SEPOY, HIS CONDUCT AND PUNISHMENT.

In venturing a few suggestions as to the most fitting punishment of our mutinous Sepoys in Bengal, I may be told at starting, "first, catch your Sepoy;" but I have sufficient confidence in the measures of the veteran General who leads our armies in the North-Western Provinces of India, to believe that the Bengal Sepoy is, sooner or later, a doomed man, and that it is merely a question of time when that doom shall overtake him. The unworthy and misguided native soldiers who have brought such infinite disgrace upon themselves, and caused so much sorrow and suffering to their employers, will ere long be dragged from their hiding places and put on their trial for mutiny and murder. What then must be their doom? This is a question, important not only as affecting the persons of some thirty or forty thousand men, the remnants of our Bengal army, but also as fixing our own future position throughout Asia. In deciding it we have in the first place to consider what is due to ourselves, as the Lords Paramount of India, and to the millions under our sway. That matter settled, we may allow the dictates of generosity to be heard.

To enter then upon this great question. The facts of the case against the criminal are unfortunately too notorious. The Sepoy of Bengal has been treated with justice and liberality. The British Government has not only shown the utmost consideration for his feelings and prejudices, but has also intrusted the public arsenals, forts, magazines, and treasuries to his keeping. In return, forgetful of the obligations of a hundred years, and without the excuse for a Prætorian career which a feeble or selfish civil Government might have afforded, the native soldier has made a blind rush at supreme power. Regiment after regiment has risen to burn and slay. In some places not a single European, man, woman or child, has escaped the fury of the soldiery. To have a white face, to wear the clothing, or even to speak the language of the Franks, has been death. The forts, providentially, have been generally held by our countrymen in spite of treachery and violence; but numerous depôts of arms and treasure in the hands of the native soldiers have supplied them on every side with the sinews of war. The jails in all directions have been attacked and thousands of prisoners set loose to assist in the work of destruction, and to carry to every village the tidings of the Englishman's disgrace. Some regiments, after falling at the feet of their officers and shedding false tears to lull suspicion, have risen suddenly by night to shoot down alike the beardless boy and the worn-out veteran. Others rushing into the quiet English homes, have put all to the bayonet. Some, as at Gwalior, have spared women and children, or only killed them as if by mistake. Others have protected their officers, and even made some show of remorse. But, with exceptions too limited to deserve much notice here, all from Meerut to Benares have deserted their colours, and proved unfaithful to their salt.

It will then be granted that the Bengal army has been guilty of mutiny, the blackest on the long list of military offences, and is punishable at discretion. A plea, however, is urged in abatement of the extreme severity of the law. The prisoner's motives, character and previous services must be considered. Let us allow due weight to the plea, and inquire what it is worth. And first as to the motive. It is urged that the Sepoy's religious prejudices have been insulted, and that this has driven him into mutiny. Now, allowing that the religious feelings of the men may have been worked upon by designing traitors, who thus sought to excuse a scheme of treachery and violence, it is only reasonable to suppose that any honest soldier who really felt himself in danger of religious defilement, would have made known his fears to his commanding officer. A respectful protest against any order offensive to caste prejudices might have been made, and then, without any real humiliation to the officers of the army, the offence might have been avoided for the future, and explained for the past.

But, such was not the conduct of the Bengal Sepoy. He has made no complaint. Accustomed to secret mutinous meetings, led on by delusive hopes of universal power, by the lust of gain and the love of plunder, he has taken advantage of the too easy confidence of his master. Temptation was before him; he yielded, and scrupled not to compass the destruction of the nation, which, for more than three generations had led his forefathers and himself to victory. We must therefore give no credit to those who seek to excuse the conduct of the Sepoy, as prompted by mere religious enthusiasm.

The truth is, that ever since the reverses at Cabool* first taught the natives of India that an English army might be annihilated, it has only been a question of time with the Sepoys when they should make Bengal, as was Cabool, the grave of the white man.

But again, the Bengal Sepoy pleads long and faithful service. The records of a century prove the truth of the first part of this plea, but it may be questioned whether length of service can constitute any apology for want of faith. It is hardly an excuse for the treacherous servant, who first stabs and then robs his master, that he has been reared from a boy in that master's house. Still, it is argued, the service rendered has been great. Now without pretending to discuss the history of the Bengal Sepoy, I think we may fairly allow that, all things considered, he has done good service. As a mercenary soldier, hired to bring or keep in subjection his own countrymen, it is our own fault if we have trusted the Sepoy too much. If we have expected of our

* I have witnessed a marked change in the conduct of the Bengal Sepoys from the period of our Cabool disasters.

armed servants, strangers to our blood and our religion, a degree of fidelity which no Indian potentate expects from his own sons, the fault is our own. The wonder is, not that the Indian soldier has been sometimes the coward, and often the bully or malingerer, but that he has so freely shed his blood in the cause of his employers, and honestly performed his duty so long amidst such great temptations. The earliest performances of Clive's 1st Regiment of Bengal Native Infantry, when first the swarthy Asiatic adopted the scarlet uniform of England, under Colonel Forde at Condore and Masulipatam, may be taken as a fair specimen of the subsequent character and conduct of the Bengal army. At Condore, to use the words of Orme, of whom it has been said by the modern Father of History *, that his narrative is one of the most authentic and one of the most finely written in our language, "the Sepoys, seeing themselves attacked, without cover, by Europeans in front, and the horse and multitude of the enemy's Sepoys gaining their rear, or coming down on their flank, scarcely preserved courage to give their fire, hurried, scattered, and without command; and then immediately broke and ran away to shelter themselves in the village of Chambole, and were followed by the nearest of the enemy's horse."†

Again, after describing the storm of Masulipatam, the same historian writes:—"The Sepoys, who behaved with equal gallantry as the Europeans, as

* Macaulay's Essays. "Life of Lord Clive."

† Book x. vol. iii. page 379.

well in the real, as at the false attacks, had about fifty killed and 150 wounded."*

In short, the Bengal Sepoy, when working with Europeans, shoulder to shoulder, has generally done well; but if unsupported has been apt to take to his heels. In some peculiar times of trial he has set a good example to European soldiers, and even to British officers. For instance, Major Coote, after the battle of Plassy, marched at the head of his Sepoys on Patna, whilst his mutinous European soldiers were ingloriously towed up the river in boats.

So again, in the days of Lord Clive, at the time of the mutiny of the British officers, it was virtually to the Sepoys that the Government had to look to keep the mass of their own officers in order.

On considering the whole case, it seems, then, that though England may not condone or pass over the crime of her mutinous Sepoys, some degree of lenity may with justice be exhibited. It is, however, of the last importance that any mildness which the British Government may practise, should not be mistaken for timidity. We may not forget the genius of the people with whom we have to deal. Moderation and power so rarely go together in their minds, that it is dangerous to yield even to those emotions of pity and generosity for a prostrate foe, which are so natural to every English breast.

The extreme rigour of the law should be enforced against every man in regiments which dyed their hands in the blood of our countrymen. In such

† Book xi. vol. iii. page 489.

cases there is no room for remorse,—justice demands the victim and mercy would be out of place.

Regiments that have gone into mutiny unattended by bloodshed, should receive a milder but still a severe punishment. If after mutiny the men of such corps in a body joined our enemies in the field, their punishment should be perpetual imprisonment, with hard labour, in transportation beyond the seas.

Lastly, men, who having deserted their colours, betook themselves quietly to their homes, should also be sent out of India, but (if I may venture a crude suggestion) rather as emigrants than convicts.* Offenders of this class might be sent to any place where the resident colonists desire to

* I make the following extracts from my journal to show the conduct of some of our troops at the time of the mutiny.

Major Raikes described the mutiny of his troops of cavalry thus:—

Hindoo Singh Kechi Russaldar (native officer of the Kechi caste, from the neighbourhood of Gwalior) told the Major not to go to the lines, for the men had sworn not to move. He and some other native officers escorted Major Raikes to within eight miles of Agra, crying and saying they were ruined; but into Agra they would not go; for, said they, all the men say we shall become Christians if we go to Agra. The Kechis were all on Major Raikes's side, but were threatened with death, to their women and children, by the Mahomedans of the regiment.

In Major Burlton's corps (also Gwalior Contingent Cavalry,) the troopers on going into mutiny actually paid the bazaar debts of an officer's servant, to the regimental sutler, to enable the man to go off with his master.

Again, Major Mackhenzie, of the 8th Irregular Cavalry, told me that his Russaldar, Mahomed Nizam (now Sirdar Buha-

have their services, and they might be declared entitled to liberty in their new homes after a certain period, say seven years of good conduct; but, neither in this case nor in any other, should a convicted mutineer be allowed to return to India. Each and all should be branded, and the punishment for escape or attempt at escape, death.

If this is severity, the reason is sufficiently obvious. If any native of India, who having once eaten of our salt, has lifted his hand against us, be permitted under the shade of his village groves to boast of his exploits against the ruling power, there is so far an end to our prestige. Either mutiny must be connected in the mind of our subjects with death, whether social or physical, or we shall have more mutinies. Severity is the truest mercy in this case, and the only safety.*

door), when a mile or two out of Bareilly in the retreat to Nynee Tal, was told by the Major to go back and look after his three motherless boys, who were left in the lines of the mutineers. The old man answered, "Give me your hand;" then looking up to heaven with tears in his eyes, he exclaimed, "I will go on with you and do my duty." I had heard of these children when I was at Futtygurh and sent to see them; they had suffered much from poverty and neglect. I would remark, once for all, that thousands of the Sepoys were driven into mutiny unwillingly by the bad characters of each corps, who killed the favourite officers in order to compromise their associates, and thus prevent the only influence which could stay the disaffection.

* The 20,000 Sepoys *detenus* in the Punjab should, as each province thoroughly settles down, be drafted gradually to their own homes.

CHAP. XV.

THE CHARACTER OF THE LATE REVOLT.

THE reader who has followed me thus far, is aware that I attribute the origin of our existing disturbances in India to a mutiny in the Bengal army, and to that cause alone; I mean that the exciting and immediate cause of the revolution is to be found in the mutiny. That we have in many parts of the country drifted from mutiny into rebellion, is too true; but I repeat my assertion, that we have to deal now with a revolt caused by a mutiny, not with a mutiny growing out of a national discontent. I shall here, with reference to the facts narrated in the earlier chapters of this work, attempt to prove the above assertion.

In the first place, I should not have offered my services to the Lieutenant-Governor to proceed to Mynpoorie as a recruiting officer, to live as I had intended in the villages of that district, unless I had positive knowledge of the good feelings of the people in May 1857.

To proceed a little later to a different part of the country, and to other native tribes, Messrs. Phillipps and Bramly, civil officers of considerable position and experience, arrived at Agra on the 10th of June, having traversed the country from

Furuckabad, and Etah in the Doab, and from Budaon in Rohilcund, with a very small escort of three or four horsemen. They had been travelling for nearly a month amongst the villages, and on their arrival at Agra declared, as I find entered in my journal, that "the villagers are all on our side, except some of the Mahomedans."

During this same entire month of June, Mr. Arthur Cocks, the Judge of Mynpoorie; Mr. Watson, the Magistrate of Allygurh; Doctor Clark, young Mr. Outram of the Civil Service, Mr. Herbert Harington, and a few others, heroically maintained their position, at or near Allygurh, after the mutiny and destruction of the station. It was because the people of the country were with and not against us, that this handful of volunteer horsemen were enabled to hold the post amidst swarms of mutineers passing up the grand trunk road to Delhi.* The same thing went on in August and September; generally wherever the Sepoys or low Mahomedan rabble were not, the English were safe. Some villagers, robbers by prescription, tradition, birth, and education, turned against us; but after the fall of Delhi, and a short taste of anarchy, the bulk of the people

* Their head-quarters were at Allygurh. When the villagers gave them notice of a large body of Sepoys coming up towards Delhi, they used at night to shift their quarters three or four miles, the mutineers at the same time often making a detour of twenty miles to avoid the volunteers. When large bodies of the Mahomedan citizens raised the green flag and swore to kill the infidels or perish in the attempt, a charge from the volunteers soon quelled their enthusiasm.

were glad to see a white face, even in the person of a revenue collector.

In order to apprehend rightly what was the feeling, as well as the conduct of the mass of the people when the mutiny broke forth, a short analysis of the component parts of the human mass in the North-Western Provinces may be useful.

The male population was divided into the following classes: —

Hindoos.	
Agricultural - - - - -	9,549,192
Non-Agricultural - - - -	4,254,453
Mahomedans.	
Agricultural - - - - -	996,950
Non-Agricultural - - - -	79,941
Total - -	16,180,536

Now, of these sixteen millions, not one-twentieth part resided in districts which had any European soldiers stationed within their limits. The mass of the people knew and acknowledged the supreme power of their English masters, but they attributed that power entirely to the bayonets of the Bengal Native Infantry, which held the forts, arsenals, and treasuries, throughout the country.

Therefore, when the native soldiers rose, as one man, to burn and slay, to pull down the halls of justice, and to break open the jails, the people at large, who knew little and thought less of the distant resources of England, concluded naturally enough that our day had gone by.

The catastrophe was viewed with very different

feelings by the various bodies of our quondam subjects.

The predatory class, the Goojurs, the Mewatties, felt instinctively that their day had come. Their natural enemy, the Magistrate, had perished at the hands of the mutineers, or was flying before them, protected only by the people over whom he lately presided. Forthwith they girded on the sword and buckler, seized the matchlock, and sallied forth to pursue their hereditary vocation of plunder. In pursuit of this instinct they played no partizan's part, but with the utmost impartiality robbed alike the straggling European running for his life, or the Sepoy carrying off his booty. As a matter of course, there was an end of police, telegraph, postal communication, and every other symptom of civilisation, wherever these harpies were found.*

The green flag of Mahomed too, had been unfurled. The mass of the followers of the false prophet rejoicing to believe that, under the auspices of the great Mogul at Delhi, their lost ascendency was to be recovered, their deep hatred to the Christian got vent, and they rushed forth to kill and destroy.

But, making deduction for these classes, the great agricultural communities, the Jat, the Brahmin, the Rajpoot, looked on the English race, under whose auspices they had so long tasted peace and security, with unfeigned compassion. Like the

* As for the telegraph, it became a favourite engine in the hands of the village marauders, who used the iron sockets (mounted on carts) as guns, and cut up the wire into slugs.

robber tribes, they considered our case hopeless, but unlike them they *at first* lamented lost order.

Such was their first impulse; they showed it in a hundred instances, by helping our straggling countrymen, and protecting them from Sepoys or rabble, often at the risk of their own lives.

But as the course of events hurried on, as Magistrate, Cutcherry, revenue process, subsided alike, these men, who, as forming the bulk of the agricultural class, had been saddled with a very full share of the public imposts, began to think it no bad change if only they could avoid revenue payments for the future.

In common with the rest of mankind they were not fond of paying taxes, nor were they long disconsolate when the tax-collector disappeared from the scene.

If there was no Government, there was no quarter-day.

It requires no special knowledge of India to comprehend the rapid spread of passive disaffection (not active hostility), under such circumstances as these.

When disaffection means more money, more power, and no taxes, its growth is a mere necessity of human nature. There would be a good crop of disaffection in Kent or Somersetshire, under parallel conditions.

But even this natural feeling yielded to a few weeks' experience of anarchy. The Zemindar soon found that it was better to pay land-tax and receive protection, than day and night to fight for his possessions with every scoundrel in the country side. And thus, the bulk of the tax-paying agricultural proprietors in the Doab, after the fall of Delhi, welcomed their English masters back with unfeigned satisfaction.

Still more did the moneyed classes, such of them at least as survived the period of anarchy, rejoice to see the English rule restored. On the retirement of the Magistrate, a furious struggle had commenced at once between the purchasers of land in possession, and the former owners. Native bankers and merchants who had long been investing their savings in land (purchased generally under decrees of court), were either murdered or scared away. The life of a capitalist in possession of land, whether as purchaser or mortgagee, was soon not worth a week's purchase. Old feuds broke out afresh, homicides, affrays, murders by day, by night, gang robberies and arson.* Things grew worse and worse, until, as I have said before, every man but the professional robber or dacoit longed for the return of the Magistrate, notwithstanding the fact that he was also the collector of the Government revenue. The robbers joined the straggling Sepoy bands, and to this day are in arms against us,

* How fare my old friends the Bhyleas? (a class of professional thieves), I asked of the Tehsildar of Shekoabad, who had come to see me at Agra in August. "Sir," he answered, "they are the most respectable class of the community left, but they are all starving." I asked why? The answer was, "When robbers are supreme, mere thieves have no chance."

whilst the rest of the people hastened to pay up all arrears of revenue into our treasuries.

Amidst these various modifications of feeling, there was one class amongst our own immediate subjects, which with a few marked exceptions adhered without a shadow of hesitation or double-dealing to our fortunes. I allude to the Talookdars, or superior holders of considerable landed estates, who received a share of the Government due, and retained some little power and influence as the fading remnants of the native landed aristocracy.*

The conduct of these men† suggests reflections

* I speak not of Oude, but of the ceded and conquered Provinces.

† It was perhaps to be expected that the Talookdars, who during the siege of Delhi had stood firm to the British Government, should, on the re-occupation of the country by us, open their mouths rather wide, whether to notify their own merits or to receive whatever the Government might think fit to drop therein. I must quote one honourable exception to this general rule in the person of my old and esteemed friend Luchmun Singh, Talookdar of Kurowlie, in the Mynpoorie district. This man had a small fort on the Grand Trunk road, near Mynpoorie. When the lamented Fletcher Hayes was murdered by his own men, Luchmun Singh secured the body, and at the risk of his own life sent it in to Mynpoorie. During the months of July and August, when continually surrounded by mutineers, he contrived to send me frequent letters concealed by his servants, sometimes in an old shoe, sometimes in a walking-stick.

After a long ride in February last, I arrived somewhat way-worn at his house. One of his servants officiously began the process of "*shampooing*" my legs; the old gentleman pushed him aside, saying, that was his privilege. Loaded with atten-

with regard to our future policy, which I shall proceed to discuss. I have, I hope, said enough here to satisfy the candid reader that we have had no rebellion, properly so called, in the North-Western Provinces of India, and that the disorganisation caused by the violence of the Sepoys and the consequent temporary withdrawal of the Magistrate, has been merely a passing evil and not a permanent lapse in our career of progress and domination.

tions, when I was starting again on my journey, I said, "What are we to do for you to show our sense of your loyal conduct?" His reply was, "I can't eat more than one dinner daily. I have seen the English back; I want nothing more."

CHAP. XVI.

OUR FUTURE RELATION TO THE PRINCES AND PEOPLE OF INDIA.

In a former chapter, I have described how the Political Agent was compelled to fly from Gwalior. Few know how much we, at Agra, are indebted to Major Macpherson for our immunity from attack by the full force of the Gwalior Contingent, with their powerful siege artillery. The real state of the case was this, the Political Agent had full influence over Scindia's Dewan, or prime minister, the celebrated Dinkur Rao.* The minister, in his turn, influenced his master, and thus Major Macpherson, from the interior of the Fort at Agra, ruled the course of events at the Court of Gwalior. Scindia, by threats, promises, cajolery, and ready money, kept the formidable Contingent Army quiet until October. When nothing could restrain them longer, he contrived to direct their progress away from his own country towards a part of the British possessions where he believed there was a sufficient force to oppose them. He continually applied to us for European soldiers to help him, and, in short, at the

* Dinkur Rao is a Bramin élève of the late Sir W. Sleeman. He is the most enlightened native that I have had the good fortune to meet.

undoubted risk of his own power and life embraced the English cause. Holkar, also, behaved faithfully and incurred equal danger for our sake. I have already noted the conduct of the Maharajah of Putialee, and might add a long list of native potentates, who, at the most critical period, risked all in their determination to stand by us. Now, but for this unexpected* devotion to our cause of the foreign powers, our difficulties would have increased indefinitely. Let us henceforth, in order to reward and confirm this fidelity, take every opportunity of declaring our distaste to any future territorial expansion, and explain to every independent or protected State in India, that we prefer faithful allies to doubtful subjects. "It will all be red," said Runjeet Singh to an officer who was pointing out the coloured line denoting British territory, "it will all be red soon." We must prove the King of Lahore wrong in this prophecy, though in the case of his own State it has already come true. I may be told that nobody wants to annex, but mere English readers can have little knowledge how zealously some of the ablest directors of the English

* Unexpected I mean in many instances. Golab Singh was well known to me, as well as his son Rhunbeer, the present King of Cashmere, as faithful friends to the British power. I was perfectly certain that they would stand by us, but did not feel the same confidence in Scindia. I remember once being cut short in an attempt to moralise at the Jummoo Palace by Golab Singh, thus: "Maharajah," I said, "the Almighty has given you great power, and I trust"——"My Almighty," interrupted the old King, "is the Company!"

press in India have advocated a career of conquest and annexation.

So much for the princes of India. This is not the place to consider the difficult questions of Contingents, Residents, &c. I merely intend to indicate the ruling principle which should hereafter guide the policy of our Indian Foreign Office.

To turn to the Home Office. Next in rank to the foreign princes of India come the Talookdars of our own provinces. Let us for a moment consider what was the position of a Talookdar, whether in the beginning of the present century in the Doab, or in the middle of the same epoch in Oude. A Talookdar, whether holding, as most of them did, large allodial rights of his own in part of his estates, or whether originally mere contractor of the Government revenue, was a very considerable person. Throughout the North-Western Provinces, at the periods of cession and conquest in the commencement of the present century, the Talookdar was treated tenderly. He was found in possession of vast tracts, often equal in area to a good-sized English county, exercising powers over the life and liberty of a teeming population, who, according to his personal character and temper, looked up to him as their tyrant or their protector. The Talookdar had palaces, forts, troops, and, in many cases, artillery, and exacted not only deference and service, but also all sorts of fines, rents, and perquisites* from his subjects. A man thus powerful

* The detail of these cesses would fill a volume ; they ex-

abroad, was not less despotic at home. If a lady of the family went astray, she was fortunate, if discovered, to get off with the loss of her nose, and generally paid the forfeit of her life.

Proud barons like these, whose authority over their people was unlimited so long as they paid a sufficient revenue to satisfy the reigning potentate, naturally clung alike to their power and their land with tenacity, and were not scrupulous as to the measures by which they increased either their power or their possessions.

A severe blow was dealt to this portion of the native aristocracy at the period of the great revenue settlement (commenced by Mr. Robert Mertins Bird, and concluded by Mr. Thomason) in the North-Western Provinces.

A methodical scrutiny into title deeds, genealogical trees, ancient imperial records, as well as into the living history of each family, whether of Talookdars, or of subordinate cultivators of the soil, disclosing, as it did, the abuse of power and opportunity, ended often in the destruction of the influence, and the diminution of the profits, of the higher class. This decadence, however, had been so long shadowed forth in the equal spirit of the laws of the East India Company, that, when the fall came, it was gradual and not unexpected. I mean that gradually we had been inculcating the doctrine of accountability of man to man, and the equality of prince and peasant in the eye of the law; and this

tended from a tax on the pregnancy of a wife to a composition on a religious head-shaving.

new doctrine prepared the Talookdars in the North-Western Provinces for the declension of their status and diminution of their estates. This sort of preparation was gradual, and the work of fifty years' administrative progress.

In Oude, however, the case was different. Under the vilest and most corrupt Administration which even Asia had ever witnessed, the power of the Talookdar had become not only despotic, but to the last degree tyrannical. The action of our British financiers on the revenue-paying classes in Oude, exemplified the legal apophthegm to the letter. "*Summum jus, summa injuria.*" Notwithstanding the remonstrances of men like George Christian, who had never been too prone to extend the powers of the native aristocracy, notwithstanding the palpable impolicy of the measure, it was determined at once and entirely to introduce that perfect equality of man and man, which though forming the just pride of Englishmen in England, could not safely be proclaimed suddenly in the latitude of Lucknow. The Talookdar class all over the country was thrown into a state of collapse. Forty years' possession was treated as nothing, if at that remote period the occupation could be proved or supposed to be proved unjust. Old ejected shareholders, trusting to the clemency and justice of the new reign, streamed from across the border back into Oude, and were at once reinstated into their privileges, or rather were endowed with beneficial interests which they had never even claimed. The women were emancipated; wives sued their husbands for liberty of conduct, village slaves dragged their lords before the petty courts, and the lowest mechanic refused the accustomed manorial perquisite or fee.

The principle of equal justice which dictated this policy was right in the abstract, but the change was introduced too rudely, too suddenly, and with too much haste.

The consequence was that when the mutiny broke out in Oude, the Talookdars rose *en masse* to assist the mutineers.

The *huk-dar's* or rightful owners, who had been placed in possession by the British Government, either surrendered at discretion to the Talookdar, and swelled his ranks, or were hunted and killed like vermin by their village lord, all over the country.

How then are we to treat the Talookdars in future? I can only suggest that without compromising the rights of our humbler and weaker subjects in Oude, we should let the Talookdar down easily, and treat him not only with justice but liberality. The extinction of this class of men is not consistent with the safety or durability of our empire, we have erred, with the best possible intentions, in paying too little heed to the position of the landed aristocracy, and our best plan is to acknowledge our error and to retrieve it. We cannot allow these men to be village tyrants, nor to be, as they desire, superior to the law, but we may make some slight concessions of our own revenue in their favour, and need not busy ourselves to hunt out and prohibit some of the least arbitrary of their manorial perquisites. We must be satisfied with a gradual improvement in the relative position of the baron and his serf, and not insist upon the instant and immediate rectification of every inveterate abuse.

Unfortunately, however, the legislator or administrator, who following the right instincts of humanity strives to improve, regenerate, and support the humbler mass of his fellow-men has in India a thankless and too often an impossible task.

The greatest happiness of the greatest number is not easily achieved, when the greatest number can or will do nothing to make themselves heard, felt, or appreciated. It is hard to help a man who resolutely declines to help himself. And here I leave the further solution of this problem to Robert Montgomery, who will do what man can do, to calm and settle the stormy ocean of politics in Oude. The danger probably now will be, not lest the Talookdars be again trampled into the dust, but lest the million be too readily restored to their (the Talookdars) ill-starred dominion.

Descending in the social scale to discuss the interests of the people at large, I can only say in a few words, what I said at some length before the mutiny.

Our intentions towards India have generally been well inspired, but the fatal error of attempting to force the policy of Europe on the people of Asia, an error which has hitherto, with one grand exception, pervaded our Indian history both military and civil, must be corrected for the future, as it has been atoned for in the past.

The divided system of Civil Government which suits the European genius, the distribution of labour and authority between the financier, the exciseman, the police, and the judicial functionary, must cease throughout India, if we really would pacify and govern the people. The Punjab system of government as introduced by Lord Dalhousie, and carried out by Sir Henry Elliot, the Lawrences, Mansel, Montgomery, Edmonstone, and Mc Leod, is so simple, so powerful, so entirely adapted to the genius of the people, that it must, like truth, prevail, and sooner or later extend over the entire Peninsula. The distinctive features of this system have been portrayed by me on another occasion,* and I believe, but for the opposition of the Legislative Council in Calcutta, that (as suggested by me and pressed on the attention, both of the local and supreme governments,) this simple system would ere now have been introduced as the basis of our future administration in the North-Western Provinces.

For the future then let us have in the person of

* I refer the reader who may wish to go further into this subject to (Appendix B.) a letter addressed by me to Mr. Ricketts. Whilst these pages are passing through the press I observe that this gentleman, who has lately taken his seat in Calcutta as Member of Council, is advocating the views I humbly suggested, and which his wide Indian experience has enabled him to test, in the Legislative Chamber. He will not find his task an easy one.

each District Chief, whether he be called Deputy-Commissioner or Magistrate and Collector, or Judge, a full and combined authority in matters of police, revenue, civil justice, and diplomacy. This is what an Asiatic can understand, but his mind can never accept the constitutional idea of a Governor.

Not to waste words further, unless we exert a despotic power in Upper India, we must leave the country and the people to the most frightful state of anarchy which the world ever saw. We cannot even try any longer to rule Asia on the constitutional principles of Europe.* Nobody dislikes the

* I have for years sighed over and protested against the absurdity of a free press amongst the natives of India. The English press has done good, and whenever guided by a spirit of patriotism instead of a systematic hostility to Government, will do more. But the native press is an abomination, above all in the eyes of the natives themselves. When I was Commissioner of Lahore, finding myself impotent to control this great evil, I proposed to Government to establish a cheap paper of useful knowledge, which I offered to edit in my own office. This failing, I was driven to the humiliating expedient of establishing cheap lithographic presses in all the jails under me, in order, if possible, to drive the native lithographs out of the market. My reason for this disgust at the native press is briefly told. Hardly a week passed but some native Sirdar or chief came to me with streaming eyes to implore me to put a stop to printed attacks made on his family affairs, which he considered ruinous to his honour. Every police or revenue official was obliged to subscribe to these ruffian prints by threats of being exposed as inefficient, corrupt, &c. Throughout India this mischief prevailed. In February 1857, a native paper addressed the public thus: "Now is the time for India to rise, with a Governor-General who has had no experience of

attempt so much as the Asiatic himself. However much philosophers may sneer, a "paternal despotism" is not only the happiest, but the only regime for India. This is not the place to say more. With a simple, firm, just system of administration, our Hindoo subjects will not only remain, as they have hitherto been, contented, but they will attach themselves to our rule, as the Sikhs, or, at all events, the Punjabees have done already. For their own happiness, as well as for our safety, the country must be disarmed at once, and for ever. The laws regarding adultery must be changed, and as in the Punjab, the adulterer of either sex be treated as a criminal. We must see the police organised, the civil courts purged, and the procedure simplified. Land should no longer be sold for ordinary debts to any decree-holder or judgment creditor, who has not as mortgagee been already placed in usufructuary possession of the soil.

The landed proprietor should no longer be expected to bear all the burdens of the State. Government should no longer fear town mobs; we have seen enough of their impotency now, and should make the trading classes take a fair share of the public imposts. Hitherto, they have enjoyed all the advantages of our settled government, and contributed nothing towards its expenses.

With a few simple changes of this nature, with an army more carefully selected from our numerous subject or allied tribes, with officers, civil

public affairs in this country, and a Commander-in-Chief who has had no experience of war in any country."

and military, fully trusted, carefully watched, and endowed with real power to punish or to reward, we may yet have a good career before us in India. Let us hope that the wounded feelings of our own countrymen may be softened by time and good management. The surest way to elicit the generous sympathies of an Englishman is to extend his powers. You secure his friendship for the native when you place the fate of the native widely under his care. A generous confidence in an English gentleman will do more to secure his hearty care of the people than any system of reports or appeals, however multiplied and complicated, can accomplish. Public officers who abuse this confidence, should at once be removed from the service.

So much for the general form and tone of our government. To revenue matters a very brief allusion will suffice.

I have already said that we should make the moneyed classes bear a share in the public burden. The Government would do well to sell their land-tax to the proprietors wherever purchasers (at twenty years' tax) can be found.* A system of paper money should be introduced. Instead of dabbling in opium manufacture, the State should tax all opium and all tobacco whilst growing in the

* Government Savings Banks should be established in every District, and, as far as possible, the existing system of making advances from the Public Treasuries to the agricultural class extended. At present, the needy Indian peasant pays the village banker fifty per cent. for an advance to buy seed; whilst his thrifty neighbour who has saved a few rupees buries them under his hut.

field. Give a wide margin to the landowners; remember Sir John Lawrence's maxim in dealing with them—"The milk that the master leaves in the cow goes to the calf." Our own prosperity depends on the prosperity of the people, and above all of the agricultural people of India.

A few words as to the Mahomedans. They have behaved, in the part of India where I had jurisdiction, very ill; so ill indeed, that if the rest of the population had sympathised with them, instead of antagonised *, I should despair of governing India for the future.

* I cannot give a fairer instance of the difference between the conduct of the Hindoo and Mahomedan people at the time of the mutiny than was afforded in our own court at Agra. We had numerous Mahomedans and Hindoos, with a small sprinkling of Christians at the bar. With one exception, all the Mahomedan pleaders left the court; one of them, Sufdur Ali by name, was hanged by order of Mr. Harington, for plundering the property of an English officer. The rest gave no assistance whatever to us. The Hindoos, on the contrary, exerted themselves to protect and secure the property of their English judges, preserved our horses and moveable property, and did whatever else they could to show their loyalty and affection. The Mahomedans either deserted us or joined the rebels. And so it was all over the north-western provinces, a Mahomedan was another word for a rebel. The only Mahomedan who behaved well amongst our pleaders in the Suddir Court was Ahmed Buxh. His history is curious. Originally a trooper in the 3rd Cavalry, the very regiment which commenced the mutiny at Meerut; he was deputed to the court to watch some cause; his extraordinary ability excited the attention of Mr. George Edminstone, at that time Registrar of the Court. He advised the trooper to give up his arms and aspire to the pleader's '*toga*.' Ahmed Buxh studied, took his diploma and certificates, and became the leader of the Agra bar. During

They have been too much trusted, and must be watched carefully hereafter. A certain portion of public appointments should be continued in their hands, proportionate to their numbers, in each district, but they should not be allowed to enjoy too large a share of the Government patronage.

At the same time that we narrowly watch their conduct, we must beware of even tacitly encouraging religious strife between them and the Hindoos. Every ebullition of religious rancour amongst the natives recoils upon ourselves. If we cannot soften we must not exasperate the jealousies of caste and religion.

To conclude, it is impossible too often to reiterate the demand for firmness and gentleness in the personal character of our Indian administrators.

If ever the iron hand in the velvet glove was wanted, it is now.

The East India Company, after placing subject nations at the foot of the Throne, after educating illustrious statesmen, and training victorious generals, is henceforth to live in history alone.

England's Sovereign* is for the first time to wield directly the sceptre of India.

the mutiny he showed such zeal for our cause, that he was accused of being a Christian, and on retiring to his own estates he still gave such aid to the magistrate as to entitle him to the marked notice and thanks of Government.

* This change, so far as it may be known to the people of India, will be hailed with respect. I say, so far as it is known, because the common people never had any very intelligent comprehension of what the Company meant. I recollect asking an intelligent yeoman, a man who paid his annual hundred

The highest aspiration of every Englishman may well be that the future administrators of our Indian empire, whilst inaugurating a bolder* and more successful policy, may, at the same time, emulate the considerate, earnest, and just traditions of the expiring dynasty.

rupees or more of revenue to the State, who the Company was, he said, "I don't know much about the matter, but '*muraroo hogee*' she is a female of some sort!"

* By boldness I mean not only that audacity without which it is impossible to succeed in Indian warfare, but also a bolder assertion of our own religion as Christians, of our own privileges as Europeans, and of our general national superiority. An Asiatic by instinct despises the man who depreciates his own position. We should legislate and govern in India as the superior race. Whenever that superiority ceases, our right to remain in India terminates also.

APPENDICES.

APPENDIX A.—FROM MR. GEORGE CHRISTIAN'S REPORT ON THE CENSUS OF THE NORTH-WESTERN PROVINCES.

General Statement No. I. Statistical Return of Land, Revenue, Area and Population, in Thirty-one Districts of the North-Western Provinces, prepared in 1852-53.

Division.	District.	Number of mouzahs or townships.	Area in square British statute miles of 640 acres each.	Area in acres.	Malgoozaree or assessed land: Cultivated acres.	Malgoozaree or assessed land: Culturable acres.	Minhaee or unassessed land: Lakhiraj acres.	Minhaee or unassessed land: Barren acres.	Demand on account of land revenue for 1851-52 in rupees.	Rate per acre on total area.	Rate per acre on total Malgoozaree.	Rate per acre on total cultivation.	Population: Hindoo: Agricultural: Male.	Population: Hindoo: Agricultural: Female.	Population: Hindoo: Non-agricultural: Male.	Population: Hindoo: Non-agricultural: Female.	Population: Mahomedans and others not Hindoo: Agricultural: Male.	Population: Mahomedans and others not Hindoo: Agricultural: Female.	Population: Mahomedans and others not Hindoo: Non-agricultural: Male.	Population: Mahomedans and others not Hindoo: Non-agricultural: Female.	Total.	Number of persons to each square British statute mile of 640 acres each.	Number of acres to each person.
1	2	3	4	5	6	7	8	9	10	11	12	13	14	15	16	17	18	19	20	21	22	23	24
Dehlie	Paneeput	338	1,583.9	812,748	402,051	261,747	19,868	134,349	8,27,133	1 0 3	1 3 9	2 0 5	94,860	78,897	49,348	38,569	20,411	16,269	31,648	44,351	389,085	306	2.09
	Hissar	653	3,294.3	2,108,279	983,823	864,609	65,528	169,799	4,65,760	0 3 6	0 4 8	0 7 5	113,874	98,170	38,556	17,207	33,686	23,183	22,044	9,075	330,852	100	6.37
	Dehlie	868	789.7	505,280	263,806	78,585	91,403	74,185	4,36,457	0 14 5	1 3 6	1 11 9	95,963	77,731	78,913	65,469	10,086	8,891	82,339	48,470	435,744	858	1.16
	Rohtuk	380	1,340.4	857,883	641,282	147,183	22,750	46,160	6,33,132	0 11 9	0 12 10	0 15 9	112,168	102,973	61,776	30,610	11,840	12,049	11,451	9,750	377,013	281	2.27
	Goorgaon	1,274	1,939.1	1,241,037	893,940	168,498	16,823	180,297	10,47,331	0 13 6	0 15 9	1 2 8	174,467	147,756	70,198	65,468	85,214	73,087	28,107	21,334	662,463	342	1.87
	Total	3,523	8,683.3	5,526,246	3,196,984	1,516,042	238,410	374,880	34,97,786	0 9 11	0 11 8	1 1 9	590,932	494,289	296,687	227,231	181,249	189,083	149,597	133,920	2,195,180	254	2.53
Meerut	Suharunpoor	1,904	2,152.3	1,383,536	774,258	211,449	34,597	348,595	10,64,513	0 12 4	1 1 9	1 6 0	166,176	109,146	183,789	125,829	53,881	44,838	73,540	67,481	801,835	370	1.73
	Moozuffurnuggur	1,123	1,646.3	1,053,641	670,658	153,173	76,987	152,713	11,07,338	1 0 10	1 5 5	1 10 10	185,478	165,368	183,973	113,563	44,286	33,007	38,672	47,075	672,861	409	1.56
	Meerut	1,832	2,201.1	1,409,063	907,758	296,091	82,093	132,856	16,33,046	1 3 3	1 7 3	1 13 10	337,105	190,650	243,614	211,683	48,996	39,834	89,336	75,098	1,185,079	516	1.94
	Bolundshuhur	1,570	1,823.4	1,167,094	715,587	149,960	85,036	220,611	10,56,835	0 14 6	1 3 8	1 7 8	152,763	136,985	154,230	149,468	34,619	33,559	49,184	47,771	778,342	427	1.50
	Allygurh	1,937	2,153.4	1,378,304	981,076	77,725	41,670	292,833	19,35,136	1 7 1	1 14 7	2 1 1	372,365	229,145	303,662	241,236	13,475	14,047	47,369	44,200	1,134,565	527	1.21
	Total	8,359	9,983.7	6,393,900	4,039,149	891,928	346,039	1,138,112	68,97,068	1 1 0	1 6 3	1 11 3	983,510	737,664	969,058	837,288	191,600	160,100	315,431	283,615	4,562,165	453	1.41
Rohilcund	Bijnore	2,030	1,900.0	1,216,005	390,825	175,533	49,026	407,234	11,96,695	0 12 9	1 3 0	2 3 2	191,219	92,796	128,227	110,202	35,613	22,921	93,135	85,878	695,291	356	1.73
	Moradabad	3,454	2,699.5	1,727,316	896,318	308,931	238,098	332,950	18,40,313	0 12 5	1 2 8	1 9 6	273,861	235,450	189,413	184,245	95,985	66,948	97,349	95,451	1,138,461	422	1.52
	Budaon	3,238	2,401.9	1,537,137	935,209	266,065	69,734	263,133	10,57,329	0 11 5	0 14 6	1 3 11	385,097	331,094	92,379	77,946	43,792	36,678	88,674	80,506	1,019,161	434	1.51
	Bareilly	3,562	3,119.1	1,996,224	1,356,361	294,810	83,680	460,393	17,69,610	0 14 3	1 3 6	1 10 9	463,647	393,784	110,787	97,189	73,640	67,921	94,481	80,989	1,378,365	448	1.45
	Shahjehanpoor	2,735	2,308.4	1,477,359	716,201	450,063	33,067	278,039	10,60,318	0 11 9	0 14 6	1 7 8	380,572	317,803	85,589	74,759	37,434	25,099	36,354	38,677	986,086	427	1.50
	Total	11,054	12,428.3	7,953,933	4,192,002	1,516,301	485,143	1,736,549	64,65,964	0 13 0	1 2 0	1 9 0	1,699,816	1,364,907	556,318	464,931	265,304	230,351	345,163	326,908	5,217,807	419	1.52
Agra	Muttra	1,019	1,618.4	1,035,349	732,363	67,394	97,349	154,307	16,57,388	1 9 9	2 0 4	2 4 5	274,285	231,850	159,452	134,829	14,004	11,909	32,825	30,511	892,509	565	1.20
	Agra	1,143	1,854.9	1,186,537	747,530	118,104	84,460	243,437	16,23,980	1 5 9	1 14 0	2 2 8	315,239	260,987	177,058	145,714	13,551	11,321	48,533	38,813	1,001,561	537	1.19
	Furruckabad	2,027	2,128.9	1,358,686	749,083	176,345	89,995	351,339	13,34,011	0 15 5	1 7 0	1 12 6	369,161	306,576	139,234	113,335	24,651	20,747	41,318	41,389	1,056,607	501	1.28
	Mynpoory	1,844	2,020.3	1,292,946	687,096	114,536	8,510	482,312	12,67,979	0 15 8	1 9 3	1 13 6	347,815	271,840	89,084	71,738	10,687	9,453	16,758	14,202	832,714	413	1.55
	Etawah	1,485	1,677.0	1,073,276	337,804	99,627	24,143	496,402	13,73,386	1 3 0	2 0 11	2 4 6	285,076	175,901	96,549	80,548	6,843	4,434	13,186	11,514	610,965	364	1.76
	Total	7,018	9,298.4	5,950,848	3,474,628	508,196	299,747	1,668,290	71,32,439	1 3 3	1 13 4	2 0 11	1,591,910	1,249,087	666,337	543,679	67,336	58,117	151,676	136,434	4,373,154	465	1.36
Allahabad	Cawnpoor	2,357	2,048.9	1,302,939	800,452	148,282	61,993	401,357	21,44,025	1 6 10	2 4 1	2 10 10	361,396	316,720	213,925	193,091	10,138	9,782	36,614	38,989	1,174,856	500	1.12
	Futtehpoor	1,577	1,583.1	1,013,171	523,753	181,985	5,427	303,006	14,26,906	1 6 6	2 3 7	2 12 9	195,357	169,809	127,108	121,179	14,435	13,371	15,904	13,640	679,767	423	1.49
	Humeerpoor	997	2,241.6	1,434,351	770,254	316,964	14,531	333,902	13,77,264	0 14 3	1 2 10	1 10 3	206,018	175,086	87,983	80,618	7,596	7,034	18,108	18,229	549,604	245	2.61
	Banda	1,857	3,006.5	1,924,119	846,821	561,981	82,384	426,066	15,91,377	0 13 3	1 3 1	1 14 1	258,153	228,162	103,835	97,341	11,872	11,176	16,256	18,686	743,672	247	2.59
	Allahabad	4,006	2,758.7	1,734,780	971,388	247,255	28,940	387,727	21,43,221	1 3 2	1 13 1	2 3 2	481,873	375,459	205,332	194,313	33,434	31,357	63,180	68,861	1,379,788	488	1.29
	Total	10,761	11,671.0	7,461,423	3,858,874	1,406,167	197,114	2,169,288	85,86,749	1 1 11	1 9 11	2 3 2	1,443,897	1,267,720	723,011	656,735	77,316	78,419	148,107	153,793	4,526,607	372	1.69
Benares	Goruckpoor	15,714	7,340.2	4,697,706	2,062,901	1,263,034	160,782	1,076,049	21,55,881	0 7 3	0 9 6	0 15 3	1,184,554	1,092,659	326,621	312,381	136,121	138,012	57,394	51,732	3,087,874	421	1.52
	Azimgurh	6,270	2,516.4	1,610,498	756,707	313,129	41,067	567,035	14,69,416	0 14 10	1 7 6	1 13 10	843,984	330,856	120,855	107,802	54,002	50,781	62,340	57,676	1,653,251	657	.97
	Jounpoor	3,481	1,552.9	993,353	578,610	38,121	26,467	332,148	13,54,056	1 4 12	1 15 9	2 3 0	442,429	378,784	108,690	101,785	23,256	20,892	36,732	34,081	1,143,749	737	.87
	Mirzapoor	3,980	5,163.3	3,307,473	708,396	263,384	1,421,419	914,370	8,83,738	0 4 1	0 10 8	1 1 6	836,134	313,986	139,825	136,793	7,806	7,458	20,736	28,850	1,104,315	214	2.93
	Benares	2,294	995.6	637,107	480,069	25,761	26,371	131,676	3,03,258	1 5 8	1 15 9	2 2 5	293,243	197,909	151,768	139,195	4,515	4,519	36,982	33,558	851,737	856	.75
	Ghazeepoor	3,088	2,161.0	1,386,808	934,994	164,168	41,883	278,924	13,08,424	1 1 2	1 6 4	1 9 11	516,598	467,739	201,883	202,339	17,687	17,268	63,158	60,061	1,596,384	738	.87
	Total	38,079	19,727.6	12,625,974	5,918,478	2,060,287	1,712,771	3,175,403	81,81,161	0 10 8	1 0 9	1 6 9	3,847,387	2,902,883	1,078,937	998,836	243,347	221,278	267,010	267,243	9,637,960	475	1.34
	Grand total	81,098	72,056.5	46,114,514	24,659,256	7,942,491	3,267,308	10,454,882	4,06,54,410	0 14 1	1 4 1	1 8 2	9,549,192	8,142,968	4,284,450	3,770,496	996,350	897,330	1,376,941	1,272,566	30,271,885	420	1.52

APPENDIX B.*

From C. Raikes, Esq., Commissioner of Lahore, and Officiating Judge in the Courts of Sudder Dewy. and Nizt. Adawlut, North-west Provinces, Agra.

To H. Ricketts, Esq., Commissioner for the Revision of Civil Salaries and Establishment throughout India.

Dated Agra: the 4th October 1856.

SIR,

I have the honour now to reply to your letter of the 30th April, and to give you my opinion on the several subjects mentioned by you. I have already informed you that as in my present office I have no time to spare from my daily duties, when the Civil Courts are open, I have been compelled to defer my reply to the present time of vacation.

2nd. Before answering *seriatim* the several questions proposed by you, and, indeed, to enable me to answer them at all in an intelligible manner, I must explain my sentiments on the form of Indian government in general.

3rd. There are two systems of government on this side of India, which may shortly be called Regulation and Non-Regulation Systems.

4th. I have served in what are called the Regulation Provinces from 1831 to 1853, and from the beginning of 1853 to the beginning of 1856, in the Non-Regulation Province of the Punjab. Lately I have again been at-

* See p. 171.

tached to the North-Western Provinces, and in a post which has enabled me to observe the general working of the system of government, and especially in the departments of Civil and Criminal Justice.

5th. In speaking of the two systems, I shall call one the Punjab, and the other the Regulation System.

6th. It would be tedious, and is unnecessary, for me here to trace the various steps which have led to the development of the government of the North-West Provinces in its existing form. But for the sake of contrast with the Punjab System, I must briefly describe the component parts of the administration in these provinces.

7th. In the North-Western Provinces there are thirty-one districts, containing a population, in round numbers, of thirty millions.

To control and administer Civil and Criminal Justice, and to collect the public Revenue in these thirty-one districts, there are six commissioners, each receiving salaries of 38,000 rupees per annum; 19 civil and sessions judges, receiving salaries of 30,000 rupees per annum each; one additional judge at 24,000 rupees per annum; and 31 civil officers holding the joint appointment of magistrate and collector on salaries of 27,000 rupees per annum. Under the magistrates and collectors are 22 joint magistrates with salaries of 12,000 rupees per annum. 10 of the same grade at 8400 rupees per annum, and (say) 40 junior assistants with average salaries of 4800 rupees per annum.

8th. Thus we have for the district local, civil administration in the North-Western Provinces (without taking into account the institutions of Government, Finance, Audit, the high Courts of Appeal, and the Revenue Board at the seat of Government), the following machinery: —

	Rupees.
6 Commissioners of Revenue and Police at - - -	228,000
19 Civil and Session Judges at -	570,000
1 additional Judge at - -	24,000
30 Magistrates and Collectors at -	810,000
2 Independent Joint Magistrates at -	24,000
20 Joint Magistrates at - -	240,000
10 Do. do. - -	84,000
40 Junior Assistants - -	192,000
Total - -	2,172,000

These appointments are held by the regularly appointed civil servants of the East India Company.

9th. The agency subordinate to Judges and Magistrates and collectors, exercising judicial functions, or acting as deputies to the collectors of districts are next shown.

Uncovenanted Deputy Collectors.

	Rupees per annum.
2 at 600 per mensem - -	14,400
20 „ 450 „ - -	108,000
8 „ 350 „ - -	33,600
15 „ 250 „ - -	45,000
Total - -	201,000

Uncovenanted Judges.

	Rupees per annum.
6 Principal Sudder Ameers at	43,200
14 do. do. do.	67,200
14 Sudder Ameers at - -	42,000
24 Moonseiffs at - - -	43,200
74 „ - - -	88,800
	284,400
Add for Uncovenanted Deputy Collectors -	201,000
Total - -	485,400

N 4

10th. We thus have a staff of Covenanted

		Rupees per ann.
Civil Servants, costing	-	- 2,172,000
Civil Servants, not Covenanted		- 485,400
Total	-	- 2,657,400

11th. In considering the administration of the North-Western Provinces, I will refer first to the Civil and Criminal jurisdiction, and then briefly to the Revenue management.

12th. Our judicial system was imported from Bengal, and rests virtually upon the code of 1793. For the regulations enacted in the beginning of the present century, for the ceded and conquered provinces, are mostly copies from those which had been promulgated at an earlier date in Bengal and Benares.

13th. It is important to bear in mind the fact that the system which wise and able men founded in one country, and in one state of society, has been introduced, with few if any modifications, into another country, and into a different state of society. For I may safely assert that the social and physical condition of the North-Western Provinces in 1856, differs very widely from what was the social and physical condition of Bengal in 1793.

14th. In Bengal sixty years ago, it was rightly considered safer and better to rely upon institutions rather than upon men. Hence, to use the words of an able modern writer, we have a judicial "system which does not depend for its success upon extraordinary individual efforts, but which is susceptible of effective superintendence and development." (Preface to Macpherson's Procedure of the Civil Courts of the East India Company.)

15th. To carry out this "strictly organised and regulated" system, we have an apparatus of highly-paid Judges, whose powers are limited to the administration of civil justice, the trial of criminal cases at the Sessions, and the hearing of appeals from orders passed by the magistrates in criminal trials.

16th. Under them again are (more or less) 125 native or other uncovenanted judges, the bulk of whom receive a very scanty salary, and who decide civil suits, giving occasional aid to the magistrate in cases of small importance in the criminal department.

17th. The salary of the judge is not much more than that of the magistrate and collector; his duties are of a description less interesting, less stirring, and on the whole more irksome. Though the judge is the superior officer in the district, the magistrate is the more important and influential personage. The magistrate is to the people the direct and powerful representative of the Government, has large patronage, and a wide discretion and power, which the judge may fetter or restrain, but cannot exercise in his own person.

18th. The result of this is, that where the judge, and the collector, and magistrate are both earnest and zealous men, there is a probability of a conflict of opinion, and a possibility of great soreness and discontent on the part of the magistrate when the judge reverses his orders.

19th. To glance hastily at the Revenue system. Here we find that the orders of the highly educated European magistrate and collector in Revenue cases, concerning rent, replevin, or ouster are liable to be revised and reversed in a regular suit before a half-educated native moonsiff, on a salary of 100 rupees per mensem. (The natives are never tired of wondering at anomalies of this sort.)

20th. Again, the magistrate and collector in Police and Revenue matters is subordinate to the Commissioner. Whatever may be the cause, the effect of the relative position of the two officers as at present regulated is not always harmony and order, and in a word, what it ought to be, subordination. It has been the generous custom of the senior members of the Civil Service to encourage freedom of opinion and discussion amongst the juniors; but this has been carried too far in many instances, and owing to this, and to the divided authority under which they labour, the magistrates and collectors, especially the more earnest men, have sometimes allowed themselves to forget the respect due to their official superiors. That such feelings have not formed the rule instead of the exception, is due to the good feeling and high principle so general in the service.

21st. I feel quite sure that the divided and remote nature of the control exercised by the judge and by the commissioner has a tendency to provoke opposition; and as the native ministerial officers and suitors, with a weakness common to their race, delight in fomenting quarrels, and in widening those breaches of courtesy which may unfortunately find place in official communications, no efforts on their part are wanting if they fancy there is an opportunity for creating or for increasing discussion.

22nd. The result of all this is, that our system of district administration, though in many respects efficient, can hardly be said to work well. There is too much friction in the component parts of the machinery, and too little unity of action. The evil-disposed intriguing part of the native population take advantage of this to set one officer or one system against another. If they cannot prosecute an enemy successfully in the criminal department, they try to harass him in the Civil Courts; if they find a magistrate or collector too active and vigorous, they endeavour to set the judge or the commissioner in opposition to him.

23rd. The idea, so natural to the European mind, that it would be unjust or impolitic for one and the same man to act as District Chief in matters of Revenue, Police, and Civil Justice, never entered into the mind of a native in India. They laugh at the division and consequent frittering away of power in the Regulation Provinces, and take advantage of the liberal and noble spirit of the Government to impede and restrict the free course of truth and justice.

24th. In a word, the natives of India are not fit, and will not be fit, to judge from the past, for centuries to come, for a Government carried on upon these principles, which suit a people who (like their rulers the British) are capable of self-government.

25th. To give them a Government on those principles is to *retard their progress*, to set the mass of the people against the ruling power, and to benefit sycophants and rogues.

26th. Social progress under the simpler *quasi* Oriental system is far more rapid than under the artificial system of checks which is established in the Regulation Provinces. I boldly assert that in the Jullunder Daob, the Lahore and Jhelum Divisions, and doubtless other parts of the Punjab, a greater progress has been made in five years than has been made in any of the Regulation Provinces in fifty. I know this to be a fact; and a reference to the Criminal Statistics of those Divisions will prove the truth of my assertion.

27th. The people there find themselves under a District Chief who has all legitimate power in his hands. Should he abuse or exceed that power, they have the Commissioner to look to for redress. The public interests of the Commissioner and of the Deputy Commissioner being identical, and the Deputy being unable (if he wished so to do) to resist the will and authority of his principal, the work goes on smoothly, harmoniously, and well. If it does not so go on, it is not the fault of the system, at all events; and my own experience is, that a Deputy Commissioner and Commissioner work together LIKE ONE MAN.

28th. My experience, on the other hand, in the Regulation Provinces is, that when an energetic, earnest Magistrate and Collector works in perfect harmony with his

Judge and Commissioner, it is owing to unusual temper and tact on the part of the subordinate, or extreme forbearance on the part of the superior officer.

29th. I therefore consider that, for India, the system introduced by our late Governor-General in the Punjab is the best.

30th. But both Commissioners and Deputy Commissioners in the Punjab are overworked and under-paid; and I therefore give below the scale of pay and the number and designation of officers which I would suggest for the North-Western Provinces,—so far as the District work is concerned.

PROPOSED SCALE OF OFFICERS AND SALARIES FOR THE NORTH-WESTERN PROVINCES, ON THE PUNJAB PLAN, MODIFIED AND IMPROVED.

Covenanted Officers.

No.	Office.	Salaries of each, per mensem.	Salaries of all, per annum.
		Rupees.	Rupees.
15	Commissioners - - -	3000	540,000
30	Deputy Commissioners - -	2000	720,000
10	Assistants, 1st grade - -	1000	120,000
20	Ditto, 2nd ditto - -	700	168,000
40	Ditto, 3rd ditto - -	400	192,000
115			1,740,000

Then for Uncovenanted Assistants.

No.	Office.	Salaries of each, per mensem.	Salaries of all, per annum.
		Rupees.	Rupees.
10	Extra Uncovenanted Assistants	600	72,000
20	Ditto - - - - - -	400	96,000
90	Ditto - - - - - -	200	216,000
120			384,000

Total Expense of District Administration in the North-West Provinces.

	Rupees.
As at present - - - - - -	2,657,000
Proposed on Punjab System - - -	2,124,000
Annual Saving by Punjab System - -	Rs. 53,300

Thus each District would have a Deputy Commissioner with two Assistants, with one Extra Assistant at 600 rs. or 400 rs. per mensem, and three Extra Assistants at 200 rs. per mensem. With this Staff, and with Tehseeldars exercising Judicial and Criminal, as well as Revenue, powers,—the Deputy Commissioner trying, in general, Appeals only (in Civil suits), and educating his first Assistant as a Judge, by giving him the heavy Judicial cases; with one Commissioner over two Deputies, who could not only support these Deputies, but also keep them in perfect order,—the work would be done with *complete despatch and efficiency*, and at a considerable saving.

31st. If the districts were thus managed and the Punjab Arms Act introduced, as it ought to be, across the length and breadth of the land, as well as a simple code of civil procedure, and a modification of the existing criminal law, there would be more order, prosperity, and internal tranquillity in Hindoostan than in any part of the world. At present we are in advance of many European countries and but little behind England in these respects. With the alterations I have sketched we should soon be unrivalled in the world. For the Indian races are amongst the most industrious, commercial, orderly, and contented people in the world, if only kept in order.

32nd. The Asiatic system of a mild despotism suits them, and it is only under a system of paternal or despotic restraint that they will ever become capable of self-improvement and consequently fit for self-government.

33rd. Intelligent, honourable, and industrious Englishmen, guided, controlled, or stimulated by the able hands of such men as have been always selected for the post of Lieutenant-Governor or Chief Commissioner in the Upper Provinces will, when free to act as in the Punjab, accomplish wonders and bring unexampled social order and commercial prosperity over the land.

34th. Such men will not waste their lives, abilities, and prospects in India on niggardly salaries such as may suffice for the judge of a county court or a stipendiary magistrate in England. Superior men will not accept inferior emoluments, and we want superior men for this work. A few able men well paid will do more for India than a larger staff of average mediocrity.

35th. The distant threats of cutting down salaries have already, I observe, taken effect; and it is notorious in England that a petty living of 200*l.* or 300*l.* per annum already holds out greater inducements to men of learning and talent than the Civil Service of India. The candidates for examination this year are far too few and only half in number of those of last year, although this year we have peace and last year were plunged in war.

36th. I need not allude to the higher offices of state held by the members of the Sudder Court and Board of Revenue at Agra, as some such machinery of government must be kept up and at the present expense. But with reference to the proposed constitution of the High Court will only express my conviction that it is a mistake, and a very dangerous one, to place natives into appointments where they will have to control European officers.

37th. I would ask whether is more of moral courage, self-reliance, candour, and intellectual light required in the office of a chief-justice or of a general of division?

38th. When natives are found fit to command our armies, brigades, or even regiments, it will be time to place them on the bench of the High Courts.

39th. They have as much physical courage as their

English rulers, are as well fitted for soldiers, but are not fit to command their own countrymen, still less are they qualified by nature or habit to command Englishmen.

40th. If then it be true, as who will doubt, that natives are unfit to command our armies, so are they equally unfitted to rule over councils, or as judges in the courts of appeal to exercise supreme control over our judicial and magisterial officers. Why should an English judge be placed under a Mahometan or Brahmin judge any more than an English colonel be put under a Brahmin general?

41st. Having ventured at some length to place before you my opinion as to the most really economical and effectual mode of district administration in these provinces I proceed to answer the queries proposed in your letter, which after the full explanation of my sentiments here given may be very briefly recorded.

42nd. *First Question.*—Would it be advantageous to introduce grades of salaries in the judicial and revenue departments? How many grades of magistrates, of collectors, of judges, and of commissioners would you have?

Answer.—I have fully answered this question in paragraphs 30 to 31, but I may add here that I think that every district chief should get a salary of 24,000 rupees per annum. If grades are introduced as a matter of economy so much the worse for the country, in my opinion. It is inconvenient to the local government to attach certain salaries to certain very large or difficult districts, because every district has its own peculiar difficulties, and the man who may be invaluable in one comparatively easy district from his local knowledge, may merit as high a salary as another officer who is selected for the charge of a very large and important district. I advocate one rate of salary of 2000 rupees per mensem for every magistrate and collector, deputy-commissioner.

43rd. *Second Question.*—Could we advantageously make further use of native agency by increasing the powers of deputy-collectors, deputy-magistrates, monlovees, pundits, moonsiffs, and tehseelders?

Answer.—Collectors can at present make over most cases, however difficult or important, to be decided by their Native Deputies. I would not increase the powers of native subordinates, as they have now, when authorised by Government, as much power as the covenanted European Deputy Collector or Joint Magistrate.

44th. *Third Question.*—Would it be advantageous to separate the Police altogether from the Magistracy and to have a Superintendent of Police in each District?

Answer.—I think it would be a step in the wrong direction to separate the Police and the Magistracy. All power in India, to suit the genius and wants of the people and their simple state of civilisation, should be placed in the same hand. The degrees of power only, and not the nature of power, should be strictly limited and defined. This is the secret of successful government in Asia.

45th. *Fourth Question.*—Would it be advisable to increase the powers of magistrates and to give them authority to pass sentence of Seven or Ten Years' Imprisonment, their notes in English, with an abstract of the case, to be forwarded for the information of the Session Judge when the sentence may exceed three years?

Answer.—If the District Chief receive a salary of 24,000 rupees, it is reasonable to suppose that he will be an officer of 10 years' standing. In that case I think it would be an improvement to increase the powers of the Magistrate in the manner here proposed.

46th. *Fifth Question.*—Does your experience tell you that to give a Session's Judge the power to set aside a Magistrate's order is productive of much mischief, and that it would be beneficial to rule that a second opinion should be taken before an order is reversed? If you think a second opinion should be taken, by what measures could a reference be most conveniently provided?

Answer.—I have already, in Paragraphs 17 to 30, shown what I consider the best remedy for the clashing between Judge and Magistrate, and Magistrate and Commissioner. The way to correct this is to give the Judge or Commissioner an identical interest, differing only in *degree* with that of the District Chief. I think that it would be better for Judges to reverse Magistrates' orders as they do now than to complicate the machinery of Government further by requiring a second opinion before a Judge could reverse. If, however, a referee be required the Commissioner should be the man. But I could never recommend so cumbersome a check.

47th. *Sixth Question.*—Could the quantity of business now carried to the Sudder Courts be advantageously diminished by the Establishment of District or Divisional Courts with a European and two Native Judges sitting together for the disposal of certain classes of cases now carried to the Sudder Courts?

Answer.—In taking up appeals from Sudder Ameers or Moonsiffs, I should not object to see two Native Judges employed instead of one. Differences of opinion to be submitted for the orders of the District Judge, whose decision would be final. I should not wish to see a European Judge and two Native Judges on the same bench.

48th. *Seventh Question.*—How could the position of Sale Ameers under regulation 1 of 1839, be improved? Should other agency for the sale of distrained property be provided, or should the power of distraint be altogether withdrawn? Would it be well to transfer the trial of summary suits to Moonsiffs, or to station Deputy Collectors in the Mofussil, with powers to try them?

Answer.—My experience only enables me to suggest, with reference to the last of these queries, that in the North-West Provinces I think it very desirable that the local government should have and exercise the power of investing the Tehseeldars with powers to try summary suits, subject to appeal to the Collector, who might make such appeals over to his Deputies, covenanted or uncovenanted. I adopted this plan in the Punjab and found it answer very well. In Bengal, where the services of Tehseeldars are not available, I presume it would be a good plan to make summary suits over to the Moonsiffs.

49th. *Eighth Question.*—Might it not be advantageous to increase the powers of Collectors and Commissioners, and to allow no appeals in cases which can be carried into the Civil Courts?

Answer.—The best plan, in my humble opinion, is that which I have sketched in Paragraphs 17 to 30 of this letter. But as it is not very probable that my suggestions will be adopted, I certainly think that it would be an improvement on the existing system if all suits for land and rent were decided entirely by the Collector and Commissioner, and were no longer preferred in the Civil Courts. This would put the agricultural interest, as such, under one set of masters.

50th. In conclusion, I beg to apologise for my own opinions thus hastily put together, by one more remark.

51st. There are, as I have remarked, two systems for Indian Government strangely growing up side by side, and each receiving daily fresh development.

The one, the *legal* or Regulation System, just in theory but unsuited in practice to the wants and genius of Asiatics. This is the system which finds favour with English lawyers, who guide the public mind of England in such questions. And this system, itself faulty, is being patched and perverted by certain pseudo-philanthropists at home who fondly believe that an English gentleman, when once landed in India, forgets the habits, instincts, and religion of his forefathers, and becomes an advocate for injustice, torture, and tyranny. These gentlemen philanthropists over-estimate the native capacity for Civil Government and for Self-Government in proportion as they undervalue the integrity, ability, and public spirit of their fellow-countrymen in India.

53rd. The other system, combining the Oriental plan, and therefore so far suiting the people, with the virtues of Christianity and so far protecting them, is the Punjab system as introduced by the Marquis of Dalhousie. The object of this scheme of government is to combine all the avowed excellencies of the Revenue System of the North-West provinces, with a sure and simple form of Civil and Criminal Justice.

54th. Officers are as far as possible well selected, well supervised, and freely trusted. They ought to be also better paid than is now the case.

55th. Under Lord Dalhousie's Government and the mixed system of English and Oriental Government, many parts of the Punjab have progressed from anarchy to civilisation at a rate which is incredible to those who have not, as I have, witnessed and examined the marvellous change.

I have the honour to be, Sir,

Your most obedient servant,

(Signed) CHARLES RAIKES.

Commr. and Supt. of Lahore, and Offig. Judge of the Sudr. Dy. and Neizt. Adwt. N. W. P. Agra.

Agra: the 4th of October, 1856.

THE END.

LIST of WORKS in GENERAL LITERATURE

PUBLISHED BY

Messrs. LONGMAN, BROWN, GREEN, LONGMANS, and ROBERTS,

39, PATERNOSTER ROW, LONDON.

CLASSIFIED INDEX.

Agriculture and Rural Affairs.

Arts, Manufactures, and Architecture.

Biography.

Books of General Utility.

Botany and Gardening.

Chronology.

Commerce and Mercantile Affairs.

Criticism, History, and Memoirs.

Geography and Atlases.

Juvenile Books.

Medicine and Surgery.

Miscellaneous and General Literature.

Natural History in general.

1-Volume Encyclopædias and Dictionaries.

Religious & Moral Works.

Poetry and the Drama.

Political Economy and Statistics.

The Sciences in general and Mathematics

Rural Sports.

Veterinary Medicine, &c.

Voyages and Travels.

Works of Fiction.

ALPHABETICAL CATALOGUE

of

NEW WORKS and NEW EDITIONS

PUBLISHED BY

Messrs. LONGMAN, BROWN, GREEN, LONGMANS, and ROBERTS,

PATERNOSTER ROW, LONDON.

Miss Acton's Modern Cookery for Private Families, reduced to a System of Easy Practice in a Series of carefully-tested Receipts, in which the Principles of Baron Liebig and other eminent Writers have been as much as possible applied and explained. Newly-revised and enlarged Edition; with 8 Plates, comprising 27 Figures, and 150 Woodcuts. Fcp. 8vo. 7s. 6d.

Acton's English Bread-Book for Do-mestic Use, adapted to Families of every grade: Containing the plainest and most minute Instructions to the Learner, and Practical Receipts for many varieties of Bread; with Notices of the present System of Adulteration and its Consequences, and of the Improved Baking Processes and Institutions established Abroad. Fcp. 8vo. price 4s. 6d. cloth.

Aikin.—Select Works of the British Poets, from Ben Jonson to Beattie. With Biographical and Critical Prefaces by Dr. AIKIN. New Edition, with Supplement by LUCY AIKIN; consisting of additional Selections from more recent Poets. 8vo. price 18s.

Arago (F.)—Biographies of Distinguished Scientific Men. Translated by Admiral W. H. SMYTH, D.C.L., F.R.S., &c.; the Rev. BADEN POWELL, M.A.; and ROBERT GRANT, M.A., F.R.A.S. 8vo. 18s.

Arago's Meteorological Essays. With an Introduction by BARON HUMBOLDT. Translated under the superintendence of Lieut.-Colonel E. SABINE, R.A., Treasurer and V.P.R.S. 8vo. 18s.

Arago's Popular Astronomy. Translated and edited by Admiral W. H. SMYTH, D.C.L., F.R.S.; and ROBERT GRANT, M.A., F.R.A.S. In Two Volumes. Vol. I. 8vo. with Plates and Woodcuts, 21s.

Arnold.—Poems. By Matthew Arnold. Third Edition of the *First Series.* Fcp. 8vo. price 5s. 6d.

Arnold.—Poems. By Matthew Arnold. Second Series, about one-third new; the rest finally selected from the Volumes of 1849 and 1852, now withdrawn. Fcp. 8vo. price 5s.

Lord Bacon's Works. A New Edition, revised and elucidated; and enlarged by the addition of many pieces not printed before Collected and Edited by ROBERT LESLIE ELLIS, M.A., Fellow of Trinity College, Cambridge; JAMES SPEDDING, M.A. of Trinity College, Cambridge; and DOUGLAS DENON HEATH, Esq., Barrister-at-Law, and late Fellow of Trinity College, Cambridge.—The publication has commenced with the Division of the *Philosophical Works*, to be completed in 5 vols., of which Vols. I. to III. in 8vo., price 18s. each, are now ready. Vols. IV. and V. are in the press.

Joanna Baillie's Dramatic and Poetical Works: Comprising the Plays of the Passions, Miscellaneous Dramas, Metrical Legends, Fugitive Pieces, and Ahalya Baee. Second Edition, with a Life of Joanna Baillie, Portrait, and Vignette. Square crown 8vo. 21s. cloth; or 42s. bound in morocco by Hayday.

Baker. — The Rifle and the Hound in Ceylon. By S. W. BAKER, Esq. New Edition, with 13 Illustrations engraved on Wood. Fcp. 8vo. 4s. 6d.

Baker. — Eight Years' Wanderings in Ceylon. By S. W. BAKER, Esq. With 6 coloured Plates. 8vo. price 15s.

Barth. — Travels and Discoveries in North and Central Africa: Being the Journal of an Expedition undertaken under the auspices of Her Britannic Majesty's Government in the Years 1849—1855. By HENRY BARTH, Ph.D., D.C.L., Fellow of the Royal Geographical and Asiatic Societies, &c. Vols. I. to III., with 11 Maps, 100 Engravings on Wood, and 36 Illustrations in tinted Lithography, price 63s.—Vols. IV. and V., completing the work, are in the press.

Bayldon's Art of Valuing Rents and Tillages, and Claims of Tenants upon Quitting Farms, at both Michaelmas and Lady-Day; as revised by Mr. DONALDSON. *Seventh Edition*, enlarged and adapted to the Present Time: With the Principles and Mode of Valuing Land and other Property for Parochial Assessment and Enfranchisement of Copyholds, under the recent Acts of Parliament. By ROBERT BAKER, Land-Agent and Valuer. 8vo. 10s. 6d.

A Month in the Forests of France. By the Hon GRANTLEY F BERKELEY, Author of *Reminiscences of a Huntsman* 8vo with 2 Etchings by John Leech (1 coloured). [*Nearly ready.*

Black's Practical Treatise on Brewing, based on Chemical and Economical Principles With Formulæ for Public Brewers, and Instructions for Private Families New Edition, with Additions. 8vo 10s. 6d.

Blaine's Encyclopædia of Rural Sports; or, a complete Account, Historical, Practical, and Descriptive, of Hunting, Shooting, Fishing, Racing, and other Field Sports and Athletic Amusements of the present day New Edition, revised by HARRY HIEOVER, EPHEMERA, and Mr A. GRAHAM With upwards of 600 Woodcuts. 8vo 50s.

Blair's Chronological and Historical Tables, from the Creation to the Present Time With Additions and Corrections from the most authentic Writers, including the Computation of St Paul, as connecting the Period from the Exode to the Temple Under the revision of SIR HENRY ELLIS, K H Imperial 8vo 31s. 6d. half-morocco.

Bloomfield. — The Greek Testament, with copious English Notes, Critical, Philological, and Explanatory. Especially adapted to the use of Theological Students and Ministers By the Rev S T BLOOMFIELD, D D, F S A Ninth Edition, revised. 2 vols 8vo with Map, price £2. 8s

Dr. Bloomfield's College and School Edition of the *Greek Testament:* With brief English Notes, chiefly Philological and Explanatory, especially formed for use in Colleges and the Public Schools Seventh Edition, improved; with Map and Index. Fcp 8vo 7s 6d.

Dr. Bloomfield's College and School *Lexicon* to the Greek Testament New Edition, carefully revised. Fcp 8vo price 10s 6d. cloth

Bourne. — A Treatise on the Steam-Engine, in its Application to Mines, Mills, Steam-Navigation, and Railways. By the Artisan Club. Edited by JOHN BOURNE, C.E. New Edition; with 33 Steel Plates and 349 Wood Engravings. 4to price 27s.

Bourne's Catechism of the Steam-Engine in its various Applications to Mines, Mills, Steam-Navigation, Railways, and Agriculture: With Practical Instructions for the Manufacture and Management of Engines of every class. Fourth Edition, enlarged; with 89 Woodcuts. Fcp. 8vo. 6s.

Bourne — A Treatise on the Screw Propeller With various Suggestions of Improvement By JOHN BOURNE, C E New Edition, thoroughly revised and corrected With 20 large Plates and numerous Woodcuts. 4to price 38s.

Boyd. — A Manual for Naval Cadets. Published with the sanction and approval of the Lords Commissioners of the Admiralty. By JOHN M'NEILL BOYD, Captain, R N With Compass-Signals in Colours, and 236 Woodcuts Fcp. 8vo 10s 6d.

Brande.—A Dictionary of Science, Literature, and Art · Comprising the History, Description, and Scientific Principles of every Branch of Human Knowledge, with the Derivation and Definition of all the Terms in general use Edited by W T BRANDE, F R S L and E, assisted by DR. J CAUVIN Third Edition, revised and corrected; with numerous Woodcuts 8vo. 60s.

Professor Brande's Lectures on Organic Chemistry, as applied to Manufactures, including Dyeing, Bleaching, Calico-Printing, Sugar-Manufacture, the Preservation of Wood, Tanning, &c, delivered before the Members of the Royal Institution Arranged by permission from the Lecturer's Notes by J SCOFFERN, M B Fcp 8vo. with Woodcuts, price 7s 6d

Brewer. — An Atlas of History and Geography, from the Commencement of the Christian Era to the Present Time Comprising a Series of Sixteen coloured Maps, arranged in Chronological Order, with Illustrative Memoirs By the Rev J S BREWER, M A, Professor of English History and Literature in King's College, London. *Second Edition,* revised and corrected Royal 8vo 12s 6d half-bound.

Brodie — Psychological Inquiries, in a Series of Essays intended to illustrate the Influence of the Physical Organisation on the Mental Faculties By SIR BENJAMIN C BRODIE, Bart Third Edition. Fcp 8vo. 5s

Bull. — The Maternal Management of Children in Health and Disease By T. BULL, M D, Member of the Royal College of Physicians, formerly Physician-Accoucheur to the Finsbury Midwifery Institution. New Edition. Fcp. 8vo 5s

Dr. T. Bull's Hints to Mothers on the Management of their Health during the Period of Pregnancy and in the Lying-in Room: With an Exposure of Popular Errors in connexion with those subjects, &c.; and Hints upon Nursing. New Edition. Fcp. 8vo. 5s.

Buckingham.—Autobiography of James Silk Buckingham: Including his Voyages, Travels, Adventures, Speculations, Successes and Failures, frankly and faithfully narrated; with Characteristic Sketches of Public Men. Vols. I. and II. post 8vo. 21s.

Bunsen. — Christianity and Mankind, their Beginnings and Prospects. By CHRISTIAN CHARLES JOSIAS BUNSEN, D.D., D.C.L., D.Ph. Being a New Edition, corrected, remodelled, and extended, of *Hippolytus and his Age.* 7 vols. 8vo. £5. 5s.

*** This Second Edition of the *Hippolytus* is composed of three distinct works, which may be had separately, as follows:—

1. Hippolytus and his Age; or, the Beginnings and Prospects of Christianity. 2 vols. 8vo. price £1. 10s.
2. Outline of the Philosophy of Universal History applied to Language and Religion: Containing an Account of the Alphabetical Conferences. 2 vols. 8vo. price £1. 13s.
3. Analecta Ante-Nicæna. 3 vols. 8vo. price £2. 2s.

Bunsen. — Lyra Germanica: Hymns for the Sundays and chief Festivals of the Christian Year. Translated from the German by CATHERINE WINKWORTH. Third Edition. Fcp. 8vo. 5s.

*** This selection of German Hymns has been made from a collection published in Germany by the Chevalier BUNSEN; and forms a companion volume to

Theologia Germanica: Which setteth forth many fair lineaments of Divine Truth, and saith very lofty and lovely things touching a Perfect Life. Translated by SUSANNA WINKWORTH. With a Preface by the Rev. CHARLES KINGSLEY; and a Letter by Chevalier BUNSEN. Third Edition. Fcp. 8vo. 5s.

Bunsen. — Egypt's Place in Universal History: An Historical Investigation, in Five Books. By C. C. J. BUNSEN, D.D., D.C.L., D.Ph. Translated from the German by C. H. COTTRELL, Esq., M.A. With many Illustrations. Vol. I. 8vo. 28s.; Vol. II. 8vo. 30s.

Burton (J. H.)—The History of Scotland from the Revolution to the Extinction of the Last Jacobite Insurrection (1689–1748). By JOHN HILL BURTON. 2 vols. 8vo. 26s.

Bishop S. Butler's General Atlas of Modern and Ancient Geography; comprising Fifty-two full-coloured Maps; with complete Indices. New Edition, nearly all re-engraved, enlarged, and greatly improved. Edited by the Author's Son. Royal 4to. 24s. half-bound.

Separately { The Modern Atlas of 28 full-coloured Maps. Royal 8vo. price 12s.
The Ancient Atlas of 24 full-coloured Maps. Royal 8vo. price 12s. }

Bishop S. Butler's Sketch of Modern and Ancient Geography. New Edition, thoroughly revised, with such Alterations introduced as continually progressive Discoveries and the latest Information have rendered necessary. Post 8vo. price 7s. 6d.

Burton.—First Footsteps in East Africa; or, an Exploration of Harar. By RICHARD F. BURTON, Captain, Bombay Army. With Maps and coloured Plates. 8vo. 18s.

Burton. — Personal Narrative of a Pilgrimage to El Medinah and Meccah. By RICHARD F. BURTON, Captain, Bombay Army. *Second Edition,* revised; with coloured Plates and Woodcuts. 2 vols. crown 8vo. price 24s.

The Cabinet Lawyer: A Popular Digest of the Laws of England, Civil and Criminal; with a Dictionary of Law Terms, Maxims, Statutes, and Judicial Antiquities; Correct Tables of Assessed Taxes, Stamp Duties, Excise Licenses, and Post-Horse Duties; Post-Office Regulations; and Prison Discipline. 17th Edition, comprising the Public Acts of the Session 1857. Fcp. 8vo. 10s. 6d.

The Cabinet Gazetteer: A Popular Exposition of All the Countries of the World; their Government, Population, Revenues, Commerce, and Industries; Agricultural, Manufactured, and Mineral Products; Religion, Laws, Manners, and Social State; With brief Notices of their History and Antiquities. By the Author of *The Cabinet Lawyer.* Fcp. 8vo. 10s. 6d. cloth; or 13s. bound in calf.

"The author has neglected no modern sources of information, and all his short, succinct, and neat descriptions of the different places are quite conformable to present knowledge. Sarawak, for example, in Borneo, is not omitted, and of San Francisco there is quite a detailed description. The work is compiled with considerable care, and in the 912 pages that it contains there is a vast amount of geographical and topographical information pleasantly condensed. The *Cabinet Gazetteer,* though not intended to supersede more elaborate works, will, to some extent, have that effect; but it will be sure to find a large and permanent circulation of its own."

ECONOMIST.

Calendar of English State Papers, Domestic Series, of the Reigns of Edward VI., Mary, Elizabeth, 1547—1580, preserved in the State Paper Department of Her Majesty's Public Record Office. Edited by ROBERT LEMON, Esq., F.S.A., under the direction of the Master of the Rolls, and with the sanction of Her Majesty's Secretary of State for the Home Department. Imperial 8vo. 15s.

Calendar of English State Papers, Domestic Series, of the Reign of James I., 1603—1610 (comprising the Papers relating to the Gunpowder Plot), preserved in the State Paper Department of H.M. Public Record Office. Edited by MARY ANNE EVERETT GREEN, Author of *The Lives of the Princesses of England,* &c., under the direction of the Master of the Rolls, and with the sanction of H.M. Secretary of State for the Home Department. Imperial 8vo. 15s.

Calvert. — The Wife's Manual; or, Prayers, Thoughts, and Songs on Several Occasions of a Matron's Life. By the Rev. W. CALVERT, M.A. Ornamented from Designs by the Author in the style of *Queen Elizabeth's Prayer-Book*. Second Edition. Crown 8vo. 10s. 6d.

Carlisle (Lord).—A Diary in Turkish and Greek Waters. By the Right Hon. the EARL OF CARLISLE. Fifth Edition. Post 8vo. price 10s. 6d.

Catlow.—Popular Conchology; or, the Shell Cabinet arranged according to the Modern System: With a detailed Account of the Animals, and a complete Descriptive List of the Families and Genera of Recent and Fossil Shells. By AGNES CATLOW. Second Edition, much improved; with 405 Woodcut Illustrations. Post 8vo. price 14s.

Cecil. — The Stud Farm; or, Hints on Breeding Horses for the Turf, the Chase, and the Road. Addressed to Breeders of Race-Horses and Hunters, Landed Proprietors, and especially to Tenant Farmers. By CECIL. Fcp 8vo. with Frontispiece, 5s.

Cecil's Stable Practice; or, Hints on Training for the Turf, the Chase, and the Road; with Observations on Racing and Hunting, Wasting, Race-Riding, and Handicapping: Addressed to Owners of Racers, Hunters, and other Horses, and to all who are concerned in Racing, Steeple-Chasing, and Fox Hunting. Fcp. 8vo. with Plate, price 5s. half-bound.

Chapman. — History of Gustavus Adolphus, and of the Thirty Years' War up to the King's Death: With some Account of its Conclusion by the Peace of Westphalia, in 1648. By B. CHAPMAN, M.A., Vicar of Letherhead. 8vo. with Plans, 12s. 6d.

Chevreul On the Harmony and Contrast of Colours, and their Applications to the Arts: Including Painting, Interior Decoration, Tapestries, Carpets, Mosaics, Coloured Glazing, Paper-Staining, Calico-Printing, Letterpress-Printing, Map-Colouring, Dress, Landscape and Flower-Gardening, &c. &c. Translated by CHARLES MARTEL. Second Edition; with 4 Plates. Crown 8vo. price 10s. 6d.

Connolly.—History of the Royal Sappers and Miners: Including the Services of the Corps in the Crimea and at the Siege of Sebastopol By T. W. J. CONNOLLY, Quartermaster of the Royal Engineers. *Second Edition*, revised and enlarged; with 17 coloured plates. 2 vols. 8vo. price 30s.

Conybeare and Howson.—The Life and Epistles of Saint Paul: Comprising a complete Biography of the Apostle, and a Translation of his Epistles inserted in Chronological Order. By the Rev. W. J. CONYBEARE, M.A.; and the Rev. J. S. HOWSON, M.A. *Second Edition*, revised and corrected; with several Maps and Woodcuts, and 4 Plates. 2 vols. square crown 8vo. 31s. 6d. cloth.

*** The Original Edition, with more numerous Illustrations, in 2 vols. 4to. price 48s.—may also be had.

Conybeare.—Essays, Ecclesiastical and Social: Reprinted, with Additions, from the *Edinburgh Review*. By the Rev. W. J. CONYBEARE, M.A., late Fellow of Trinity College, Cambridge. 8vo. 12s.

Dr. Copland's Dictionary of Practical Medicine: Comprising General Pathology, the Nature and Treatment of Diseases, Morbid Structures, and the Disorders especially incidental to Climates, to Sex, and to the different Epochs of Life; with numerous approved Formulæ of the Medicines recommended. Vols. I. and II. 8vo. price £3; and Parts X. to XVIII. 4s. 6d. each.

*** Part XIX, completing the work, is nearly ready.

Cotton.—Instructions in the Doctrine and Practice of Christianity. Intended chiefly as an Introduction to Confirmation. By G. E. L. COTTON, M.A. 18mo. 2s. 6d.

Cresy's Encyclopædia of Civil Engineering, Historical, Theoretical, and Practical. Illustrated by upwards of 3,000 Woodcuts. *Second Edition*, revised and brought down to the Present Time in a Supplement, comprising Metropolitan Water-Supply, Drainage of Towns, Railways, Cubical Proportion, Brick and Iron Construction, Iron Screw Piles, Tubular Bridges, &c. 8vo. 63s. cloth. — The SUPPLEMENT separately, price 10s. 6d. cloth.

The Cricket-Field; or, the Science and History of the Game of Cricket. By the Author of *Principles of Scientific Batting*. Second Edition, greatly improved; with Plates and Woodcuts. Fcp. 8vo. price 5s.

Crosse.—Memorials, Scientific and Literary, of Andrew Crosse, the Electrician. Edited by Mrs. CROSSE. Post 8vo. 9s. 6d.

Cruikshank. — The Life of Sir John Falstaff, illustrated by George Cruikshank. With a Biography of the Knight, from authentic sources, by ROBERT B. BROUGH, Esq. Royal 8vo.—In course of publication monthly, and to be completed in 10 Numbers, each containing 2 Plates, price 1s. The first 6 Numbers are now ready.

Lady Cust's Invalid's Book.—The Invalid's Own Book: A Collection of Recipes from various Books and various Countries. By the Honourable LADY CUST. *Second Edition*. Fcp. 8vo. price 2s. 6d.

Dale.—The Domestic Liturgy and Family Chaplain, in Two Parts: PART I. Church Services adapted for Domestic Use, with Prayers for Every Day of the Week, selected from the Book of Common Prayer; PART II. an appropriate Sermon for Every Sunday in the Year. By the Rev. THOMAS DALE, M.A., Canon Residentiary of St. Paul's. Second Edition. Post 4to. 21s. cloth; 31s. 6d. calf; or £2. 10s. morocco.

Separately { THE FAMILY CHAPLAIN, 12s. / THE DOMESTIC LITURGY, 10s. 6d.

Davy (Dr. J.)—The Angler and his Friend; or, Piscatory Colloquies and Fishing Excursions. By JOHN DAVY, M.D., F.R.S., &c. Fcp. 8vo. price 6s.

The Angler in the Lake District: Or, Piscatory Colloquies and Fishing Excursions in Westmoreland and Cumberland. By JOHN DAVY, M.D., F.R.S. Fcp. 8vo. 6s. 6d.

Delabeche.—Report on the Geology of Cornwall, Devon, and West Somerset. By SIR H. T. DELABECHE, F.R.S. With Maps, Plates, and Woodcuts. 8vo. price 14s.

De la Rive.—A Treatise on Electricity in Theory and Practice. By A. DE LA RIVE, Professor in the Academy of Geneva. Translated for the Author by C. V. WALKER, F.R.S. *In Three Volumes*; with numerous Woodcuts. Vol. I. 8vo. price 18s.; Vol. II. price 28s.—Vol. III. is in the press.

De Vere.—May Carols. By Aubrey de VERE, Author of *The Search after Prosperine*, &c. Fcp. 8vo. 5s.

Discipline. By the Author of "Letters to my Unknown Friends," &c. Second Edition, enlarged. 18mo. price 2s. 6d.

Dodd.—The Food of London: A Sketch of the chief Varieties, Sources of Supply, probable Quantities, Modes of Arrival, Processes of Manufacture, suspected Adulteration, and Machinery of Distribution of the Food for a Community of Two Millions and a Half. By GEORGE DODD, Author of *British Manufactures*, &c. Post 8vo. 10s. 6d.

Estcourt.—Music the Voice of Harmony in Creation. Selected and arranged by Mary Jane Estcourt. Fcp. 8vo. 7s. 6d.

The Eclipse of Faith; or, a Visit to a Religious Sceptic. *8th Edition*. Fcp. 8vo. 5s.

Defence of The Eclipse of Faith, by its Author: Being a Rejoinder to Professor Newman's *Reply*: Including a full Examination of that Writer's Criticism on the Character of Christ; and a Chapter on the Aspects and Pretensions of Modern Deism. *Second Edition*, revised. Post 8vo. 5s. 6d.

The Englishman's Greek Concordance of the New Testament: Being an Attempt at a Verbal Connexion between the Greek and the English Texts; including a Concordance to the Proper Names, with Indexes, Greek-English and English-Greek. New Edition, with a new Index. Royal 8vo. price 42s.

The Englishman's Hebrew and Chaldee Concordance of the Old Testament: Being an Attempt at a Verbal Connexion between the Original and the English Translations; with Indexes, a List of the Proper Names and their Occurrences, &c. 2 vols. royal 8vo. £3. 13s. 6d.; large paper, £4. 14s. 6d.

Ephemera's Handbook of Angling; teaching Fly-Fishing, Trolling, Bottom-Fishing, Salmon-Fishing: With the Natural History of River-Fish, and the best Modes of Catching them. Third Edition, corrected and improved; with Woodcuts. Fcp. 8vo. 5s.

Ephemera.—The Book of the Salmon: Comprising the Theory, Principles, and Practice of Fly-Fishing for Salmon; Lists of good Salmon Flies for every good River in the Empire; the Natural History of the Salmon, its Habits described, and the best way of artificially Breeding it. By EPHEMERA; assisted by ANDREW YOUNG. Fcp. 8vo. with coloured Plates, price 14s.

Fairbairn.—Useful Information for Engineers: Being a Series of Lectures delivered to the Working Engineers of Yorkshire and Lancashire. With Appendices, containing the Results of Experimental Inquiries into the Strength of Materials, the Causes of Boiler Explosions, &c. By WILLIAM FAIRBAIRN, F.R.S., F.G.S. *Second Edition*; with numerous Plates and Woodcuts. Crown 8vo. price 10s. 6d.

The Fairy Family: A Series of Ballads and Metrical Tales illustrating the Fairy Mythology of Europe. With Frontispiece and Pictorial Title. Crown 8vo. 10s. 6d.

Flemish Interiors. By the Writer of *A Glance behind the Grilles of Religious Houses in France*. Fcp. 8vo. 7s. 6d.

Forester.—Travels in the Islands of Corsica and Sardinia. By THOMAS FORESTER, Author of *Rambles in Norway.* With numerous coloured Illustrations and Woodcuts, from Sketches made during the Tour by Lieutenant-Colonel M. A. BIDDULPH, R.A. Imperial 8vo. [*In the press.*

Garratt.—Marvels and Mysteries of Instinct; or, Curiosities of Animal Life. By GEORGE GARRATT. *Second Edition*, revised and improved; with a Frontispiece. Fcp. 8vo. 4s. 6d.

Gilbart.—A Practical Treatise on Banking. By JAMES WILLIAM GILBART, F.R.S., General Manager of the London and Westminster Bank. *Sixth Edition*, revised and enlarged. 2 vols. 12mo. Portrait, 16s.

Gilbart. — Logic for the Million: A Familiar Exposition of the Art of Reasoning. By J. W. GILBART, F.R.S. 5th Edition; with Portrait of the Author. 12mo. 3s. 6d.

The Poetical Works of Oliver Goldsmith. Edited by BOLTON CORNEY, Esq. Illustrated by Wood Engravings, from Designs by Members of the Etching Club. Square crown 8vo. cloth, 21s.; morocco, £1. 16s.

Gosse. — A Naturalist's Sojourn in Jamaica. By P. H. GOSSE, Esq. With Plates. Post 8vo. price 14s.

Green.—Lives of the Princesses of England. By Mrs. MARY ANNE EVERETT GREEN, Editor of the *Letters of Royal and Illustrious Ladies.* With numerous Portraits. Complete in 6 vols. post 8vo. price 10s. 6d. each.—Any Volume may be had *separately* to complete sets.

Mr. W. R. Greg's Essays on Political and Social Science, contributed chiefly to the *Edinburgh Review.* 2 vols. 8vo. price 24s.

Greyson. — Selections from the Correspondence of R. E. H. GREYSON, Esq. Edited by the Author of *The Eclipse of Faith.* 2 vols. fcp. 8vo. price 12s.

Grove. — The Correlation of Physical Forces. By W. R. GROVE, Q.C., M.A., F.R.S., &c. *Third Edition.* 8vo. price 7s.

Gurney.—St. Louis and Henri IV.: Being a Second Series of Historical Sketches. By the Rev. JOHN H. GURNEY, M.A., Rector of St. Mary's, Marylebone. Fcp. 8vo. 6s.

Evening Recreations; or, Samples from the Lecture-Room. Edited by the Rev. J. H. GURNEY, M.A. Crown 8vo. 5s.

Gwilt's Encyclopædia of Architecture, Historical, Theoretical, and Practical. By JOSEPH GWILT. With more than 1,000 Wood Engravings, from Designs by J. S. GWILT. Third Edition. 8vo. 42s.

Halloran.—Eight Months' Journal kept on board one of H.M. Sloops of War, during Visits to Loochoo, Japan, and Pootoo. By ALFRED L. HALLORAN, Master, R.N. With Etchings and Woodcuts. Post 8vo. 7s. 6d.

Hare (Archdeacon).—The Life of Luther, in Forty-eight Historical Engravings. By GUSTAV KONIG. With Explanations by ARCHDEACON HARE and SUSANNA WINKWORTH. Fcp. 4to. price 28s.

Harford.—Life of Michael Angelo Buonarroti: With Translations of many of his Poems and Letters; also Memoirs of Savonarola, Raphael, and Vittoria Colonna. By JOHN S. HARFORD, Esq., D.C.L., F.R.S., Member of the Academy of Painting of St. Luke, at Rome, and of the Roman Archæological Society. With Portrait and Plates. 2 vols. 8vo. 25s.

Illustrations, Architectural and Pictorial, of the Genius of Michael Angelo Buonarroti. With Descriptions of the Plates, by the Commendatore CANINA; C. R. COCKERELL, Esq., R.A.; and J. S. HARFORD, Esq., D.C.L., F.R.S. Folio, 73s. 6d. half-bound.

Harrison.—The Light of the Forge; or, Counsels drawn from the Sick-Bed of E. M. By the Rev. W. HARRISON, M.A., Domestic Chaplain to H.R.H. the Duchess of Cambridge. Fcp. 8vo. price 5s.

Harry Hieover.—Stable Talk and Table Talk; or, Spectacles for Young Sportsmen. By HARRY HIEOVER. New Edition, 2 vols. 8vo. with Portrait, price 24s.

Harry Hieover.—The Hunting-Field. By HARRY HIEOVER. With Two Plates. Fcp. 8vo. 5s. half-bound.

Harry Hieover. — Practical Horsemanship. By HARRY HIEOVER. *Second Edition*; with 2 Plates. Fcp. 8vo. 5s. half-bound.

Harry Hieover.—The Pocket and the Stud; or, Practical Hints on the Management of the Stable. By HARRY HIEOVER. Second Edition; with Portrait of the Author. Fcp. 8vo. price 5s. half-bound.

Harry Hieover.—The Stud, for Practical Purposes and Practical Men: Being a Guide to the Choice of a Horse for use more than for show. By HARRY HIEOVER. With 2 Plates. Fcp. 8vo. price 5s. half-bound.

Hassall.—Adulterations Detected; or, Plain Instructions for the Discovery of Frauds in Food and Medicine. By ARTHUR HILL HASSALL, M.D. Lond., Analyst of *The Lancet* Sanitary Commission, and Author of the Reports of that Commission published under the title of *Food and its Adulterations* (which may also be had, in 8vo. price 28s.) With 225 Illustrations, engraved on Wood. Crown 8vo. 17s. 6d.

Hassall.—A History of the British Fresh Water Algæ: Including Descriptions of the Desmideæ and Diatomaceæ. With upwards of One Hundred Plates of Figures, illustrating the various Species. By ARTHUR HILL HASSALL, M.D., Author of *Microscopic Anatomy of the Human Body*, &c. 2 vols. 8vo. with 103 Plates, price £1. 15s.

Col. Hawker's Instructions to Young Sportsmen in all that relates to Guns and Shooting. 10th Edition, revised and brought down to the Present Time, by the Author's Son, Major P. W. L. HAWKER. With a Portrait of the Author, and numerous Plates and Woodcuts. 8vo. 21s.

Haydn's Book of Dignities: Containing Rolls of the Official Personages of the British Empire, Civil, Ecclesiastical, Judicial, Military, Naval, and Municipal, from the Earliest Periods to the Present Time. Together with the Sovereigns of Europe, from the Foundation of their respective States; the Peerage and Nobility of Great Britain; &c. Being a New Edition, improved and continued, of Beatson's Political Index. 8vo. 25s. half-bound.

Sir John Herschel.—Essays from the *Edinburgh* and *Quarterly Reviews*, with Addresses and other Pieces. By SIR JOHN F. W. HERSCHEL, Bart., K.H., M.A. 8vo. price 18s.

Sir John Herschel.—Outlines of Astronomy. By SIR JOHN F. W. HERSCHEL, Bart., K.H., M.A. New Edition; with Plates and Woodcuts. 8vo. price 18s.

Hill.—Travels in Siberia. By S. S. Hill, Esq., Author of *Travels on the Shores of the Baltic.* With a large Map of European and Asiatic Russia. 2 vols. post 8vo. 24s.

Hinchliff.—Summer Months among the Alps: With the Ascent of Monte Rosa. By THOMAS W. HINCHLIFF, of Lincoln's Inn, Barrister-at-Law. With 4 tinted Views and 3 Maps. Post 8vo. price 10s. 6d.

Hints on Etiquette and the Usages of Society: With a Glance at Bad Habits. New Edition, revised (with Additions) by a Lady of Rank. Fcp 8vo. price Half-a-Crown.

Holland.—Medical Notes and Reflections. By SIR HENRY HOLLAND, Bart., M.D., F.R.S., &c., Physician in Ordinary to the Queen and Prince Albert. Third Edition. 8vo. 18s.

Holland.—Chapters on Mental Physiology. By SIR HENRY HOLLAND, Bart., F.R.S., &c. Founded chiefly on Chapters contained in the First and Second Editions of *Medical Notes and Reflections* by the same Author. 8vo. price 10s. 6d.

Hook.—The Last Days of Our Lord's Ministry: A Course of Lectures on the principal Events of Passion Week. By the Rev. W. F. HOOK, D.D. New Edition. Fcp. 8vo. price 6s.

Hooker.—Kew Gardens; or, a Popular Guide to the Royal Botanic Gardens of Kew. By SIR WILLIAM JACKSON HOOKER, K.H., &c., Director. New Edition; with many Woodcuts. 16mo. price Sixpence.

Hooker.—Museum of Economic Botany; or, a Popular Guide to the Useful and Remarkable Vegetable Products of the Museum in the Royal Gardens of Kew. By SIR W. J. HOOKER, K.H., &c., Director. With 29 Woodcuts. 16mo. price 1s.

Hooker and Arnott.—The British Flora; comprising the Phænogamous or Flowering Plants, and the Ferns. Seventh Edition, with Additions and Corrections; and numerous Figures illustrative of the Umbelliferous Plants, the Composite Plants, the Grasses, and the Ferns. By SIR W. J. HOOKER, F.R.A. and L.S., &c.; and G. A. WALKER-ARNOTT, LL.D., F.L.S. 12mo. with 12 Plates, price 14s.; with the Plates coloured, price 21s.

Horne's Introduction to the Critical Study and Knowledge of the Holy Scriptures. *Tenth Edition*, revised, corrected, and brought down to the present time. Edited by the Rev. T. HARTWELL HORNE, B.D. (the Author); the Rev. SAMUEL DAVIDSON, D.D. of the University of Halle, and LL.D.; and S. PRIDEAUX TREGELLES, LL.D. With 4 Maps and 22 Vignettes and Facsimiles. 4 vols. 8vo. £3. 13s. 6d.

*** The Four Volumes may also be had *separately* as follows:—

VOL. I.—A Summary of the Evidence for the Genuineness, Authenticity, Uncorrupted Preservation, and Inspiration of the Holy Scriptures. By the Rev. T. H. Horne, B.D. . 8vo. 15s.

VOL. II.—The Text of the *Old Testament* considered: With a Treatise on Sacred Interpretation; and a brief Introduction to the *Old Testament* Books and the *Apocrypha.* By S. Davidson, D.D. (Halle) and LL D. . . . . 8vo. 25s.

VOL. III.—A Summary of Biblical Geography and Antiquities. By the Rev. T. H. Horne, B.D. . . . . 8vo. 18s.

VOL. IV.—An Introduction to the Textual Criticism of the *New Testament.* By the Rev. T. H. Horne, B.D. The Critical Part re-written, and the remainder revised and edited by S. P. Tregelles, LL.D. . . . . 8vo. 18s.

Horne. — A Compendious Introduction to the Study of the Bible. By the Rev. T. HARTWELL HORNE, B.D. New Edition, with Maps and Illustrations. 12mo. 9s.

Hoskyns.—Talpa; or, the Chronicles of a Clay Farm: An Agricultural Fragment. By CHANDOS WREN HOSKYNS, Esq. Fourth Edition. With 24 Woodcuts from the original Designs by GEORGE CRUIKSHANK. 16mo. price 5s. 6d.

How to Nurse Sick Children: Intended especially as a Help to the Nurses in the Hospital for Sick Children; but containing Directions of service to all who have the charge of the Young. Fcp. 8vo. 1s. 6d.

Howitt (A. M.)—An Art-Student in Munich. By ANNA MARY HOWITT. 2 vols. post 8vo. price 14s.

Howitt.—The Children's Year. By Mary HOWITT. With Four Illustrations, from Designs by A. M. HOWITT. Square 16mo. 5s.

Howitt.—Tallangetta, the Squatter's Home: A Story of Australian Life. By WILLIAM HOWITT, Author of *Two Years in Victoria,* &c. 2 vols. post 8vo. price 18s.

Howitt.—Land, Labour, and Gold; or, Two Years in Victoria: With Visit to Sydney and Van Diemen's Land. By WILLIAM HOWITT. 2 vols. post 8vo. 21s.

Howitt.—Visits to Remarkable Places: Old Halls, Battle-Fields, and Scenes illustrative of Striking Passages in English History and Poetry. By WILLIAM HOWITT. With about 80 Wood Engravings. *New Edition.* 2 vols. square crown 8vo. price 25s.

William Howitt's Boy's Country Book: Being the Real Life of a Country Boy, written by himself; exhibiting all the Amusements, Pleasures, and Pursuits of Children in the Country. New Edition; with 40 Woodcuts. Fcp. 8vo. price 6s.

Howitt.—The Rural Life of England. By WILLIAM HOWITT. New Edition, corrected and revised; with Woodcuts by Bewick and Williams. Medium 8vo. 21s.

Huc.—Christianity in China, Tartary, and Thibet. By M. l'Abbé HUC, formerly Missionary Apostolic in China; Author of *The Chinese Empire,* &c. 2 vols. 8vo. 21s.

Huc.—The Chinese Empire: A Sequel to Huc and Gabet's *Journey through Tartary and Thibet.* By the Abbé HUC, formerly Missionary Apostolic in China. *Second Edition;* with Map. 2 vols. 8vo. 24s.

Hudson's Plain Directions for Making Wills in conformity with the Law: With a clear Exposition of the Law relating to the distribution of Personal Estate in the case of Intestacy, two Forms of Wills, and much useful information. New and enlarged Edition; including the Provisions of the Wills Act Amendment Act. Fcp. 8vo. 2s. 6d.

Hudson's Executor's Guide. New and improved Edition; with the Statutes enacted, and the Judicial Decisions pronounced since the last Edition incorporated, comprising the Probate and Administration Acts for England and Ireland, passed in the first Session of the New Parliament. Fcp. 8vo. [*Just ready.*

Hudson and Kennedy.—Where there's a Will there's a Way: An Ascent of Mont Blanc by a New Route and Without Guides. By the Rev. C. HUDSON, M.A., St. John's College, Cambridge; and E. S. KENNEDY, B.A., Caius College, Cambridge. *Second Edition,* with Two Ascents of *Monte Rosa;* a Plate, and a coloured Map. Post 8vo. 5s. 6d.

Humboldt's Cosmos. Translated, with the Author's authority, by MRS. SABINE. Vols. I. and II. 16mo. Half-a-Crown each, sewed; 3s. 6d. each, cloth: or in post 8vo. 12s. each, cloth. Vol. III. post 8vo. 12s. 6d. cloth: or in 16mo. Part I. 2s. 6d. sewed, 3s. 6d. cloth; and Part II. 3s. sewed, 4s. cloth.

Humboldt's Aspects of Nature. Translated, with the Author's authority, by MRS. SABINE. 16mo. price 6s.: or in 2 vols. 3s. 6d. each, cloth; 2s. 6d. each, sewed.

Humphreys. — Parables of Our Lord, illuminated and ornamented in the style of the Missals of the Renaissance by HENRY NOEL HUMPHREYS. Square fcp. 8vo. 21s. in massive carved covers; or 30s. bound in morocco by Hayday.

Hunt. — Researches on Light in its Chemical Relations; embracing a Consideration of all the Photographic Processes. By ROBERT HUNT, F.R.S. Second Edition, with Plate and Woodcuts. 8vo. 10s. 6d.

Hutton.—A Hundred Years Ago: An Historical Sketch, 1755 to 1756. By JAMES HUTTON. Post 8vo.

Idle.—Hints on Shooting, Fishing, &c., both on Sea and Land, and in the Fresh-Water Lochs of Scotland: Being the Experiences of C. IDLE, Esq. Fcp. 8vo. 5s.

Mrs. Jameson's Legends of the Saints and Martyrs, as represented in Christian Art: Forming the First Series of *Sacred and Legendary Art.* Third Edition, revised and improved; with 17 Etchings and upwards of 180 Woodcuts, many of which are new in this Edition. 2 vols. square crown 8vo. 31s. 6d.

Mrs. Jameson's Legends of the Monastic Orders, as represented in Christian Art. Forming the Second Series of *Sacred and Legendary Art.* Second Edition, enlarged; with 11 Etchings by the Author, and 88 Woodcuts. Square crown 8vo. price 28s.

Mrs. Jameson's Legends of the Madonna, as represented in Christian Art: Forming the Third Series of *Sacred and Legendary Art.* Second Edition, revised and improved: with numerous Etchings from Drawings by the Author, and upwards of 150 Woodcuts. Square crown 8vo. [*Nearly ready.*

Mrs. Jameson's Commonplace-Book of Thoughts, Memories, and Fancies, Original and Selected. Part I. Ethics and Character; Part II. Literature and Art. *Second Edit.* revised and corrected; with Etchings and Woodcuts. Crown 8vo. 18s.

Mrs. Jameson's Two Lectures on the Employment of Women.

1. Sisters *of* Charity, Catholic and Protestant, Abroad and at Home *Second Edition*, with new Preface Fcp. 8vo 4s
2. *The* Communion *of* Labour A Second Lecture on the Social Employments of Women. Fcp. 8vo. 3s.

Jaquemet's Compendium of Chronology: Containing the most important Dates of General History, Political, Ecclesiastical, and Literary, from the Creation of the World to the end of the Year 1854. Edited by the Rev. J. Alcorn, M.A. *Second Edition.* Post 8vo. price 7s. 6d.

Lord Jeffrey's Contributions to The Edinburgh Review. A New Edition, complete in One Volume, with a Portrait engraved by Henry Robinson, and a Vignette. Square crown 8vo. 21s. cloth; or 30s. calf. —Or in 3 vols. 8vo. price 42s.

Bishop Jeremy Taylor's Entire Works: With Life by Bishop Heber. Revised and corrected by the Rev. Charles Page Eden, Fellow of Oriel College, Oxford. Now complete in 10 vols. 8vo. 10s. 6d. each.

Johns.—The Land of Silence and the Land of Darkness. Being Two Essays on the Blind and on the Deaf and Dumb. By the Rev. B. G. Johns, Chaplain of the Blind School, St. George's Fields, Southwark. Fcp. 8vo. price 4s 6d.

Johnston.—A Dictionary of Geography, Descriptive, Physical, Statistical, and Historical: Forming a complete General Gazetteer of the World. By A. Keith Johnston, F.R.S.E., F.R.G.S., F.G.S., Geographer at Edinburgh in Ordinary to Her Majesty. Second Edition, thoroughly revised. In 1 vol. of 1,360 pages, comprising about 50,000 Names of Places. 8vo. 36s. cloth; or half-bound in russia, 41s.

Kemble.—The Saxons in England: A History of the English Commonwealth till the Norman Conquest. By John M. Kemble, M.A., &c. 2 vols. 8vo. 28s.

Kesteven.—A Manual of the Domestic Practice of Medicine. By W. B. Kesteven, Fellow of the Royal College of Surgeons of England, &c. Square post 8vo. 7s. 6d.

Kirby and Spence's Introduction to Entomology; or, Elements of the Natural History of Insects: Comprising an Account of Noxious and Useful Insects, of their Metamorphoses, Food, Stratagems, Habitations, Societies, Motions, Noises, Hybernation, Instinct, &c. *Seventh Edition*, with an Appendix relative to the Origin and Progress of the work. Crown 8vo. 5s.

Mrs. R. Lee's Elements of Natural His-tory; or, First Principles of Zoology: Comprising the Principles of Classification, interspersed with amusing and instructive Accounts of the most remarkable Animals. New Edition; Woodcuts. Fcp. 8vo. 7s. 6d.

Letters to my Unknown Friends. By a Lady, Author of *Letters on Happiness.* Fourth Edition. Fcp. 8vo. 5s.

Letters on Happiness, addressed to a Friend. By a Lady, Author of *Letters to my Unknown Friends.* Fcp. 8vo 6s.

L.E.L.—The Poetical Works of Letitia Elizabeth Landon; comprising the *Improvisatrice*, the *Venetian Bracelet*, the *Golden Violet*, the *Troubadour*, and Poetical Remains. New Edition; with 2 Vignettes by R. Doyle. 2 vols. 16mo. 10s. cloth; morocco, 21s.

Dr. John Lindley's Theory and Practice of Horticulture; or, an Attempt to explain the principal Operations of Gardening upon Physiological Grounds: Being the Second Edition of the *Theory of Horticulture*, much enlarged; with 98 Woodcuts. 8vo. 21s.

Dr. John Lindley's Introduction to Botany. New Edition, with Corrections and copious Additions. 2 vols. 8vo. with Six Plates and numerous Woodcuts, price 24s.

Loudon's Encyclopædia of Plants: Comprising the Specific Character, Description, Culture, History, Application in the Arts, and every other desirable Particular respecting all the Plants found in Great Britain. New Edition, corrected by MRS. LOUDON. With upwards of 12,000 Woodcuts. 8vo. £3. 13s. 6d.—Second Supplement, 21s.

Loudon's Encyclopædia of Cottage, Farm, and Villa Architecture and Furniture. New Edition, edited by MRS. LOUDON; with more than 2,000 Woodcuts. 8vo. 63s.

Loudon's Self-Instruction for Young Gardeners, Foresters, Bailiffs, Land Stewards, and Farmers; in Arithmetic, Bookkeeping, Geometry, Mensuration, Practical Trigonometry, Mechanics, Land-Surveying, Levelling, Planning and Mapping, Architectural Drawing, and Isometrical Projection and Perspective. 8vo. Portrait, 7s. 6d.

Loudon's Hortus Britannicus; or, Catalogue of all the Plants found in Great Britain. New Edition, corrected by MRS. LOUDON. 8vo. 31s. 6d.

Mrs. Loudon's Lady's Country Companion; or, How to Enjoy a Country Life Rationally. Fourth Edition, with Plates and Woodcuts. Fcp. 8vo. 5s.

Mrs. Loudon's Amateur Gardener's Calendar, or Monthly Guide to what should be avoided and done in a Garden. 16mo. with Woodcuts, 7s. 6d.

Low's Elements of Practical Agriculture; comprehending the Cultivation of Plants, the Husbandry of the Domestic Animals, and the Economy of the Farm. New Edition; with 200 Woodcuts. 8vo. 21s.

Macaulay.—Speeches of the Right Hon. Lord Macaulay. Corrected by HIMSELF. 8vo. price 12s.

Macaulay.—The History of England from the Accession of James II. By the Right Hon. LORD MACAULAY. New Edition. Vols. I. and II. 8vo. price 32s.; Vols III. and IV. price 36s.

Lord Macaulay's Critical and Historical Essays contributed to The Edinburgh Review. Four Editions, as follows:—

1. A LIBRARY EDITION (the *Eighth*), in 3 vols. 8vo. price 36s.
2. Complete in ONE VOLUME, with Portrait and Vignette. Square crown 8vo. price 21s. cloth; or 30s. calf.
3. Another NEW EDITION, in 3 vols. fcp. 8vo. price 21s. cloth.
4. The PEOPLE'S EDITION, in 2 vols. crown 8vo. price 8s. cloth.

Macaulay.—Lays of Ancient Rome, with *Ivry* and the *Armada*. By the Right Hon. LORD MACAULAY. New Edition. 16mo. price 4s. 6d. cloth; or 10s. 6d. bound in morocco.

Lord Macaulay's Lays of Ancient Rome. With numerous Illustrations, Original and from the Antique, drawn on Wood by George Scharf, jun., and engraved by Samuel Williams. New Edition. Fcp. 4to. price 21s. boards; or 42s. bound in morocco.

Mac Donald. — Poems. By George MAC DONALD, Author of *Within and Without*. Fcp. 8vo. 7s.

Mac Donald.—Within and Without: A Dramatic Poem. By GEORGE MAC DONALD. *Second Edition*, revised; fcp. 8vo. 4s. 6d.

Macdonald. — Villa Verocchio; or, the Youth of Leonardo da Vinci: A Tale. By the late MISS D. L. MACDONALD. Fcp. 8vo. price 6s.

MacDougall.—The Theory of War illus-trated by numerous Examples from History. By Lieutenant-Colonel MACDOUGALL, Superintendent of Studies in the Royal Military College, Sandhurst. Post 8vo. with 10 Plans of Battles, price 10s. 6d.

M'Dougall.—The Eventful Voyage of *H.M. Discovery Ship* Resolute *to the Arctic Regions in Search of Sir John Franklin and the Missing Crews of H.M. Discovery Ships* Erebus *and* Terror, 1852, 1853, 1854. To which is added an Account of her being fallen in with by an American Whaler, after her abandonment in Barrow Straits, and of her presentation to Queen Victoria by the Government of the United States. By GEORGE F. M'DOUGALL, Master. With a coloured Chart; 8 Illustrations in tinted Lithography; and 22 Woodcuts. 8vo. price 21s. cloth.

Sir James Mackintosh's Miscellaneous Works: Including his Contributions to The Edinburgh Review. Complete in One Volume; with Portrait and Vignette. Square crown 8vo. 21s. cloth; or 30s. bound in calf: or in 3 vols. fcp. 8vo. 21s.

Sir James Mackintosh's History of England from the Earliest Times to the final Establishment of the Reformation. Library Edition, revised. 2 vols. 8vo. 21s.

Macleod.—The Theory and Practice of Banking: With the Elementary Principles of Currency, Prices, Credit, and Exchanges. By HENRY DUNNING MACLEOD, of the Inner Temple, Esq., Barrister-at-Law. 2 vols. royal 8vo. price 30s.

Macnaught.—The Doctrine of Inspiration: Being an Inquiry concerning the Infallibility, Inspiration, and Authority of Holy Writ. By the Rev. JOHN MACNAUGHT, M.A. *Second Edition*, revised. Crown 8vo. price 4s. 6d.

M'Culloch's Dictionary, Practical, Theoretical, and Historical, of Commerce and Commercial Navigation. Illustrated with Maps and Plans. New Edition, corrected to the Present Time; with a Supplement. 8vo. price 50s. cloth; half-russia, 55s.

M'Culloch's Dictionary, Geographical, Statistical, and Historical, of the various Countries, Places, and principal Natural Objects in the World. Illustrated with Six large Maps. New Edition, revised; with a Supplement. 2 vols 8vo. price 63s.

Maguire.—Rome; its Ruler and its Institutions. By JOHN FRANCIS MAGUIRE, M.P. With a Portrait of Pope Pius IX. Post 8vo. price 10s. 6d.

Maitland.—The Church in the Catacombs: A Description of the Primitive Church of Rome. Illustrated by its Sepulchral Remains. By the Rev. CHARLES MAITLAND. New Edition; with several Woodcuts. 8vo. price 14s.

Out-of-Doors Drawing.—Aphorisms on Drawing. By the Rev. S. C MALAN, M.A. of Balliol College, Oxford; Vicar of Broadwindsor, Dorset. Post 8vo. 3s. 6d.

Mrs. Marcet's Conversations on Chemistry, in which the Elements of that Science are familiarly explained and illustrated by Experiments. New Edition, enlarged and improved. 2 vols. fcp. 8vo. price 14s.

Mrs. Marcet's Conversations on Natural Philosophy, in which the Elements of that Science are familiarly explained. New Edition, enlarged and corrected; with 23 Plates. Fcp. 8vo. price 10s. 6d.

Martineau.—Endeavours after the Christian Life: Discourses. By JAMES MARTINEAU. 2 vols. post 8vo. 7s. 6d. each.

Martineau.—Hymns for the Christian Church and Home. Collected and edited by JAMES MARTINEAU. *Eleventh Edition*, 32mo. 3s 6d. cloth, or 5s calf; *Fifth Edition*, 32mo. 1s. 4d. cloth, or 1s. 8d roan.

Martineau.—Miscellanies: Comprising Essays on Dr Priestley, Arnold's *Life and Correspondence*, Church and State, Theodore Parker's *Discourse of Religion*, "Phases of Faith," the Church of England, and the Battle of the Churches. By JAMES MARTINEAU. Post 8vo. 9s.

Maunder's Scientific and Literary Treasury: A new and popular Encyclopædia of Science and the Belles-Lettres; including all branches of Science, and every subject connected with Literature and Art. New Edition. Fcp. 8vo. price 10s. cloth; bound in roan, 12s.; calf, 12s. 6d.

Maunder's Biographical Treasury; consisting of Memoirs, Sketches, and brief Notices of above 12,000 Eminent Persons of All Ages and Nations, from the Earliest Period of History: Forming a new and complete Dictionary of Universal Biography. Ninth Edition, revised throughout. Fcp. 8vo. 10s. cloth; bound in roan, 12s.; calf, 12s. 6d.

Maunder's Treasury of Knowledge, and Library of Reference. Comprising an English Dictionary and Grammar, a Universal Gazetteer, a Classical Dictionary, a Chronology, a Law Dictionary, a Synopsis of the Peerage, numerous useful Tables, &c. New Edition, carefully revised and corrected throughout: With Additions. Fcp. 8vo. 10s. cloth; bound in roan, 12s.; calf, 12s. 6d.

Maunder's Treasury of Natural History; or, a Popular Dictionary of Animated Nature: In which the Zoological Characteristics that distinguish the different Classes, Genera, and Species, are combined with a variety of interesting Information illustrative of the Habits, Instincts, and General Economy of the Animal Kingdom. With 900 Woodcuts. New Edition. Fcp. 8vo. price 10s. cloth; roan, 12s.; calf, 12s. 6d.

Maunder's Historical Treasury; comprising a General Introductory Outline of Universal History, Ancient and Modern, and a Series of separate Histories of every principal Nation that exists; their Rise, Progress, and Present Condition, the Moral and Social Character of their respective Inhabitants, their Religion, Manners and Customs, &c. New Edition; revised throughout, with a new GENERAL INDEX. Fcp. 8vo. 10s. cloth; roan, 12s.; calf, 12s. 6d.

Maunder's Geographical Treasury.— The Treasury of Geography, Physical, Historical, Descriptive, and Political; containing a succinct Account of Every Country in the World. Preceded by an Introductory Outline of the History of Geography; a Familiar Inquiry into the Varieties of Race and Language exhibited by different Nations; and a View of the Relations of Geography to Astronomy and the Physical Sciences. Commenced by the late SAMUEL MAUNDER; completed by WILLIAM HUGHES, F.R G.S., late Professor of Geography in the College for Civil Engineers. *New Edition*; with 7 Maps and 16 Steel Plates. Fcp. 8vo. 10s. cloth; roan, 12s.; calf, 12s. 6d.

Melville. — The Confidence-Man: His Masquerade. By Herman Melville, Author of *Typee, Omoo,* &c. Fcp. 8vo. 5s.

Merivale. — A History of the Romans under the Empire. By the Rev. Charles Merivale, B.D., late Fellow of St. John's College, Cambridge. 8vo. with Maps.

Vols. I. and II. comprising the History to the Fall of *Julius Cæsar*. Second Edition............................28s.
Vol. III. to the establishment of the Monarchy by *Augustus*. Second Edition..............................14s.
Vols. IV. and V. from *Augustus* to *Claudius*, B.C. 27 to A.D. 54...32s.

Merivale.—The Fall of the Roman Republic: A Short History of the Last Century of the Commonwealth. By the Rev. C. Merivale, B.D , late Fellow of St. John's College, Cambridge. New Edition. 12mo. 7s. 6d.

Merivale.—An Account of the Life and Letters of Cicero. Translated from the German of Abeken; and Edited by the Rev. Charles Merivale, B.D. 12mo. 9s. 6d.

Merivale (L. A.)—Christian Records: A Short History of Apostolic Age. By L. A. Merivale. Fcp. 8vo. 7s. 6d.

Miles.—The Horse's Foot, and How to Keep it Sound. *Eighth Edition*; with an Appendix on Shoeing in general, and Hunters in particular, 12 Plates and 12 Woodcuts. By W. Miles, Esq. Imperial 8vo. 12s. 6d.

*** Two Casts or Models of Off Fore Feet, No. 1, *Shod for All Purposes*, No. 2, *Shod with Leather*, on Mr. Miles's plan, may be had, price 3s. each.

Miles.—A Plain Treatise on Horse-Shoeing. By William Miles, Esq. With Plates and Woodcuts. Small 4to. price 5s.

Milner's History of the Church of Christ. With Additions by the late Rev. Isaac Milner, D D., F.R.S. A New Edition, revised, with additional Notes by the Rev. T. Grantham, B.D. 4 vols. 8vo. price 52s.

Montgomery.—Memoirs of the Life and Writings of James Montgomery: Including Selections from his Correspondence, Remains in Prose and Verse, and Conversations. By John Holland and James Everett. With Portraits and Vignettes. 7 vols. post 8vo. price £3. 13s. 6d.

James Montgomery's Poetical Works: Collective Edition; with the Author's Autobiographical Prefaces, complete in One Volume; with Portrait and Vignette. Square crown 8vo. price 10s. 6d. cloth; morocco, 21s.—Or, in 4 vols. fcp. 8vo. with Portrait, and 7 other Plates, price 14s.

Moore.—The Power of the Soul over the Body, considered in relation to Health and Morals. By George Moore, M.D. *Fifth Edition.* Fcp. 8vo. 6s.

"It shows that unless the inward principle be disciplined, purified, and enlightened, vainly must we look for that harmony between mind and body so necessary to human enjoyment.....We would say, Read the book."
ATHENÆUM.

Moore.—Man and his Motives. By George Moore, M.D. *Third Edition.* Fcp. 8vo. 6s.

Moore.—The Use of the Body in relation to the Mind. By George Moore, M.D. *Third Edition.* Fcp. 8vo. 6s.

Moore. — Memoirs, Journal, and Correspondence of Thomas Moore. Edited by the Right Hon. Lord John Russell, M.P. With Portraits and Vignette Illustrations. 8 vols. post 8vo. price 10s. 6d. each.

Thomas Moore's Poetical Works: Comprising the Author's recent Introductions and Notes. The *Traveller's Edition*, complete in One Volume, printed in Ruby Type; with a Portrait. Crown 8vo. 12s 6d. cloth; morocco by Hayday, 21s.—Also the *Library Edition* complete in 1 vol. medium 8vo. with Portrait and Vignette, 21s. cloth; morocco by Hayday, 42s.—And the *First collected Edition*, in 10 vols. fcp. 8vo. with Portrait and 19 Plates, price 35s.

Moore. — Poetry and Pictures from Thomas Moore. Being Selections of the most popular and admired of Moore's Poems, copiously illustrated with highly-finished Wood Engravings from original Designs by

C. W. Cope, R.A.	F. R. Pickersgill, R.A.
E. C. Corbould,	S. Read,
J. Cropsey,	G. Thomas,
E. Duncan,	F. Topham,
Birket Foster,	H. Warren,
J. C. Horsley, A.R.A.	Harrison Weir, and
H. Le Jeune,	F. Wyburd.

Fcp. 4to., printed on toned paper, and elegantly bound. [*Nearly ready.*

Moore's Epicurean. New Edition, with the Notes from the collective edition of *Moore's Poetical Works*; and a Vignette engraved on Wood from an original Design by D. Maclise, R.A. 16mo. 5s. cloth; or 12s. 6d. morocco by Hayday.

Moore's Songs, Ballads, and Sacred Songs. New Edition, printed in Ruby Type; with the Notes from the collective edition of *Moore's Poetical Works*, and a Vignette from a Design by T. Creswick, R.A. 32mo. 2s. 6d.—An Edition in 16mo. with Vignette by R. Doyle, price 5s.; or 12s. 6d. morocco by Hayday.

Moore's Lalla Rookh: An Oriental Romance. With 13 highly-finished Steel Plates from Original Designs by Corbould, Meadows, and Stephanoff, engraved under the superintendence of the late Charles Heath. New Edition. Square crown 8vo. price 15s. cloth; morocco, 28s.

Moore's Lalla Rookh. New Edition, printed in Ruby Type; with the Preface and Notes from the collective edition of *Moore's Poetical Works*, and a Frontispiece from a Design by Kenny Meadows. 32mo. 2s. 6d. —An Edition in 16mo. with Vignette, 5s.; or 12s. 6d. morocco by Hayday.

Moore's Irish Melodies. A New Edition, with 13 highly-finished Steel Plates, from Original Designs by

C. W. COPE, R.A.	D. MACLISE, R.A.
T. CRESWICK, R.A.	J. E. MILLAIS, A.R.A.
A. L. EGG, A.R.A.	W. MULREADY, R.A.
W. P. FRITH, R.A.	J. SANT,
W. E. FROST, A.R.A.	F. STONE, A.R.A.; and
J. C. HORSLEY,	E. M. WARD, R.A.

Square crown 8vo. price 21s. cloth; or 31s. 6d. handsomely bound in morocco.

Moore's Irish Melodies, printed in Ruby Type; with the Preface and Notes from the collective edition of *Moore's Poetical Works*, the Advertisements originally prefixed, and a Portrait of the Author. 32mo. 2s. 6d.—An Edition in 16mo. with Vignette, 5s.; or 12s. 6d. morocco by Hayday.

Moore's Irish Melodies. Illustrated by D. Maclise, R.A. New Edition; with 161 Designs, and the whole of the Letterpress engraved on Steel, by F. P. Becker. Super-royal 8vo. 31s. 6d. boards; £2. 12s. 6d. morocco by Hayday.

Moore's Irish Melodies, the Music with the Words; the Symphonies and Accompaniments by Sir John Stevenson, Mus. Doc. Complete in One Volume, small Music size, convenient and legible at the pianoforte, but more portable than the usual form of Musical publications. Imperial 8vo. 31s. 6d. cloth; or 42s. half-bound in morocco.

Moore.—The Crosses, Altar, and Ornaments in the Churches of St. Paul's, Knightsbridge, and St. Barnabas, Pimlico: A concise Report of the Proceedings and Judgments in the Cases of Westerton *v.* Liddell, Horne, and others, and Beal *v.* Liddell, Parke, and Evans; as heard and determined by the Consistory Court of London, the Arches Court of Canterbury, and the Judicial Committee of H.M. Most Hon. Privy Council. By EDMUND F. MOORE, Esq., M.A., Barrister-at-Law. Royal 8vo. price 12s. cloth.

Morell.—Elements of Psychology: Part I, containing the Analysis of the Intellectual Powers. By J. D. MORELL, M.A., One of Her Majesty's Inspectors of Schools. Post 8vo. 7s. 6d.

Morning Clouds. [A book of practical ethics, in form of letters of counsel, encouragement, and sympathy, specially addressed to young women on their entrance into life.] Post 8vo. price 7s.

Moseley.—The Mechanical Principles of Engineering and Architecture. By H. MOSELEY, M.A., F.R.S., Canon of Bristol, &c. Second Edition, enlarged; with numerous Corrections and Woodcuts. 8vo. 24s.

Memoirs and Letters of the late Colonel ARMINE S. H. MOUNTAIN, C.B., Aide-de-Camp to the Queen, and Adjutant-General of Her Majesty's Forces in India. Edited by Mrs. MOUNTAIN. With a Portrait drawn on Stone by R. J. LANE, A.E.R.A. Post 8vo 8s. 6d.

Mure.—A Critical History of the Language and Literature of Ancient Greece. By WILLIAM MURE, M.P. of Caldwell. Second Edition. Vols. I. to III. 8vo. price 36s.; Vol. IV. price 15s.; Vol. V. price 18s.

Murray's Encyclopædia of Geography; comprising a complete Description of the Earth: Exhibiting its Relation to the Heavenly Bodies, its Physical Structure, the Natural History of each Country, and the Industry, Commerce, Political Institutions, and Civil and Social State of All Nations. Second Edition; with 82 Maps, and upwards of 1,000 other Woodcuts. 8vo. price 60s.

Neale.—The Closing Scene; or, Christianity and Infidelity contrasted in the Last Hours of Remarkable Persons. By the Rev. ERSKINE NEALE, M.A. New Editions. 2 vols. fcp. 8vo. price 6s. each.

Oldacre.—The Last of the Old Squires. A Sketch. By CEDRIC OLDACRE, Esq., of Sax-Normanbury, sometime of Christ Church, Oxon. Crown 8vo. price 9s. 6d.

Osborn.—Quedah; or, Stray Leaves from a Journal in Malayan Waters. By Captain SHERARD OSBORN, R.N., C.B., Author of *Stray Leaves from an Arctic Journal*, and of the *Narrative of the Discovery of the North-West Passage*. With a coloured Chart and tinted Illustrations. Post 8vo. price 10s. 6d.

Osborn.—The Discovery of the North-West Passage by H.M.S. *Investigator*, Captain R. M'Clure, 1850-1854. Edited by Captain Sherard Osborn, C.B., from the Logs and Journals of Captain R. M'Clure. Second Edition, revised; with Additions to the Chapter on the Hybernation of Animals in the Arctic Regions, a Geological Paper by Sir Roderick I. Murchison, a Portrait of Captain M'Clure, a coloured Chart and tinted Illustrations. 8vo. price 15s.

Owen.—Lectures on the Comparative Anatomy and Physiology of the Invertebrate Animals, delivered at the Royal College of Surgeons. By Richard Owen, F.R.S., Hunterian Professor to the College. Second Edition, with 235 Woodcuts. 8vo. 21s.

Professor Owen's Lectures on the Comparative Anatomy and Physiology of the Vertebrate Animals, delivered at the Royal College of Surgeons in 1844 and 1846. With numerous Woodcuts. Vol. I. 8vo. price 14s.

Memoirs of Admiral Parry, the Arctic Navigator. By his Son, the Rev. E. Parry, M.A. of Balliol College, Oxford; Domestic Chaplain to the Lord Bishop of London. Third Edition; with a Portrait and coloured Chart of the North-West Passage. Fcp. 8vo. price 5s.

Dr. Pereira's Elements of Materia Medica and Therapeutics. *Third Edition*, enlarged and improved from the Author's Materials, by A. S. Taylor, M.D., and G. O. Rees, M.D.: With numerous Woodcuts. Vol. I. 8vo. 28s.; Vol. II. Part I. 21s.; Vol. II. Part II. 24s.

Dr. Pereira's Lectures on Polarised Light, together with a Lecture on the Microscope. 2d Edition, enlarged from Materials left by the Author, by the Rev. B. Powell, M.A., &c. Fcp. 8vo. with Woodcuts, 7s.

Perry.—The Franks, from their First Appearance in History to the Death of King Pepin. By Walter C. Perry, Barrister-at-Law, Doctor in Philosophy and Master of Arts in the University of Gottingen. 8vo. price 12s. 6d.

Peschel's Elements of Physics. Translated from the German, with Notes, by E. West. With Diagrams and Woodcuts. 3 vols. fcp. 8vo. 21s.

Ida Pfeiffer's Lady's Second Journey round the World: From London to the Cape of Good Hope, Borneo, Java, Sumatra, Celebes, Ceram, the Moluccas &c., California, Panama, Peru, Ecuador, and the United States. 2 vols. post 8vo. 21s.

Phillips's Elementary Introduction to Mineralogy. A New Edition, with extensive Alterations and Additions, by H. J. Brooke, F.R.S., F.G.S.; and W. H. Miller, M.A., F.G.S. With numerous Wood Engravings. Post 8vo. 18s.

Phillips.—A Guide to Geology. By John Phillips, M.A., F.R.S., F.G.S., &c. Fourth Edition, corrected to the Present Time; with 4 Plates. Fcp. 8vo. 5s.

Phillips.—Figures and Descriptions of the Palæozoic Fossils of Cornwall, Devon, and West Somerset; observed in the course of the Ordnance Geological Survey of that District. By John Phillips, F.R.S., F.G.S., &c. 8vo. with 60 Plates, price 9s.

Piesse's Art of Perfumery, and Methods of Obtaining the Odours of Plants: With Instructions for the Manufacture of Perfumes for the Handkerchief, Scented Powders, Odorous Vinegars, Dentifrices, Pomatums, Cosmétiques, Perfumed Soap, &c.; and an Appendix on the Colours of Flowers, Artificial Fruit Essences, &c. *Second Edition*, revised and improved; with 46 Woodcuts. Crown 8vo. 8s. 6d.

Captain Portlock's Report on the Geology of the County of Londonderry, and of Parts of Tyrone and Fermanagh, examined and described under the Authority of the Master-General and Board of Ordnance. 8vo. with 48 Plates, price 24s.

Powell.—Essays on the Spirit of the Inductive Philosophy, the Unity of Worlds, and the Philosophy of Creation. By the Rev. Baden Powell, M.A., F.R.S., F.R.A.S., F.G.S., Savilian Professor of Geometry in the University of Oxford. Second Edition, revised. Crown 8vo. with Woodcuts, 12s. 6d.

Pycroft's Course of English Reading, adapted to every taste and capacity: With Literary Anecdotes. New and cheaper Edition. Fcp. 8vo. price 5s.

Raikes.—A Portion of the Journal kept by Thomas Raikes, Esq., from 1831 to 1847: Comprising Reminiscences of Social and Political Life in London and Paris during that period. Vols. I. and II. (*Second Edition*), post 8vo. 21s.; Vols. III. and IV. with *Index*, completing the work, price 21s.

Reade.—The Poetical Works of John Edmund Reade. New Edition, revised and corrected; with Additional Poems. 4 vols. fcp. 8vo. price 20s.

Dr. Reece's Medical Guide: Comprising a complete Modern Dispensatory, and a Practical Treatise on the distinguishing Symptoms, Causes, Prevention, Cure, and Palliation of the Diseases incident to the Human Frame. Seventeenth Edition, corrected and enlarged by the Author's Son, Dr. H. Reece, M.R.C.S., &c. 8vo. 12s.

Rich's Illustrated Companion to the Latin Dictionary and Greek Lexicon: Forming a Glossary of all the Words representing Visible Objects connected with the Arts, Manufactures, and Every-Day Life of the Ancients. With about 2,000 Woodcuts from the Antique. Post 8vo. 21s.

Richardson.—Fourteen Years' Experience of Cold Water: Its Uses and Abuses. By Captain M. Richardson, late of the 4th Light Dragoons. Post 8vo. with Woodcuts, price 6s.

"The first object of Captain Richardson's book is to extend the use of the cold-water cure to the humbler classes, by a simpler mode of treatment. This simplicity principally consists in the substitution of wet bandages covered by dry bandages for the wet sheet and other processes of established hydropathy. Captain Richardson considers the bandage not only more beneficial medically than the sheet, but much more easily applied, while it does not interrupt a man's avocations, but can be worn even at work. The general expositions are followed by directions for the treatment of diseases under the Captain's system." Spectator.

Horsemanship; or, the Art of Riding and Managing a Horse, adapted to the Guidance of Ladies and Gentlemen on the Road and in the Field: With Instructions for Breaking-in Colts and Young Horses. By Captain Richardson, late of the 4th Light Dragoons. With 5 Plates. Square crown 8vo. 14s.

Household Prayers for Four Weeks; With additional Prayers for Special Occasions. To which is added a Course of Scripture Reading for Every Day in the Year. By the Rev. J. E. Riddle, M.A., Incumbent of St. Philip's, Leckhampton. Crown 8vo. price 3s. 6d.

Riddle's Complete Latin-English and English-Latin Dictionary, for the use of Colleges and Schools. *New* and cheaper *Edition*, revised and corrected. 8vo. 21s.

Separately { The English-Latin Dictionary, 7s. / The Latin-English Dictionary, 15s.

Riddle's Diamond Latin-English Dictionary. A Guide to the Meaning, Quality, and right Accentuation of Latin Classical Words. Royal 32mo. price 4s.

Riddle's Copious and Critical Latin-English Lexicon, founded on the German-Latin Dictionaries of Dr. William Freund. New *and cheaper* Edition. Post 4to. 31s. 6d.

Rivers's Rose-Amateur's Guide; coing ample Descriptions of all the fine varieties of Roses, regularly classed respective Families; their Histo Mode of Culture. Fifth Edition, co and improved. Fcp. 8vo. 3s. 6d.

Dr. E. Robinson's Greek and E Lexicon to the Greek Testament. Edition, revised and in great part re- 8vo. price 18s.

Mr. Henry Rogers's Essays selecte Contributions to the *Edinburgh* Second *and cheaper* Edition, with Ad 3 vols. fcp. 8vo. 21s.

Dr. Roget's Thesaurus of English and Phrases classified and arranged facilitate the Expression of Ideas an in Literary Composition. Sixth E revised and improved. Crown 8vo. 1

Ronalds's Fly-Fisher's Entom With coloured Representations Natural and Artificial Insect, and a f servations and Instructions on Tro Grayling Fishing. *Fifth Edition*, thor revised by an Experienced Fly-Fisher 20 new coloured Plates. 8vo. 14s.

Rowton's Debater: A Series of com Debates, Outlines of Debates, and Qu for Discussion; with ample Reference best Sources of Information. New E Fcp. 8vo. 6s.

The Saints our Example. By the A of *Letters to my Unknown Friends*, &c. 8vo. price 7s.

Scherzer.—Travels in the Free Sta Central America: Nicaragua, Hon and San Salvador. By Dr. Carl Sch With a coloured Map. 2 vols. post 8v

"Central America is not an inviting place for the lounging traveller. The roads are bad; there are no inns; food is scarce; the people are dishonest; scoundrels swarm; neither life nor property is safe. Dr. Scherzer travelled with guides of doubtful fidelity, was forced to keep his hand on his gun and revolver, sometimes compelled to eat a few black beans or starve; now groping at night through a forest, now escorted by barefooted soldiers with helmets of pasteboard a now swinging in a h in a filthy hovel; ceiving the Preside State by the light of stuck in a bottle. A having a hard and h life of it. But he complain. A chee braver traveller seld made his way in ou tracks far beyond th of the civilised wor The Central Americ tion will probably en Scherzer's book wit ditional attraction." G

Dr. L. Schmitz's History of Greece, the Earliest Times to the Taking of C by the Romans, B.C. 146, mainly base Bishop Thirlwall's History. *Fourth E* with Supplementary Chapters on the rature and the Arts of Ancient Greec illustrated with a Map of Athens an Woodcuts, designed from the Antiq G. Scharf, jun., F.S.A. 12mo. 7s. 6d

Scrivenor's History of the Iron Trade, from the Earliest Records to the Present Period. New Edition, corrected. 8vo. price 10s. 6d.

Sir Edward Seaward's Narrative of his Shipwreck, and consequent Discovery of certain Islands in the Caribbean Sea. Third Edition. 2 vols. post 8vo. 21s.—An ABRIDGMENT, in 16mo. price 2s. 6d.

The Sermon in the Mount. Printed by C. Whittingham, uniformly with the *Thumb Bible;* bound and clasped. 64mo. 1s. 6d.

Sewell.—Amy Herbert. By a Lady. Edited by the Rev. WILLIAM SEWELL, B.D., Fellow and Tutor of Exeter College, Oxford. New Edition. Fcp. 8vo. price 6s.

Sewell.—The Earl's Daughter. By the Author of *Amy Herbert.* Edited by the Rev. W. SEWELL, B.D. 2 vols. fcp. 8vo. 9s.

Sewell.—Gertrude: A Tale. By the Author of *Amy Herbert.* Edited by the Rev. W. SEWELL, B.D. Fcp. 8vo. price 6s.

Sewell.—Margaret Percival. By the Author of *Amy Herbert.* Edited by the Rev. W. SEWELL, B.D. 2 vols. fcp. 8vo. price 12s.

By the same Author, New Editions,

Ivors. 2 vols. fcp. 8vo. price 12s.

Cleve Hall. 2 vols. fcp. 8vo. price 12s.

Katharine Ashton. 2 vols. fcp. 8vo. 12s.

The Experience of Life. Fcp. 8vo. price 7s. 6d.

Laneton Parsonage: A Tale for Children, on the Practical Use of a portion of the Church Catechism. 2 vols. fcp. 8vo. price 12s.

Readings for Every Day in Lent: Compiled from the Writings of BISHOP JEREMY TAYLOR. Fcp. 8vo. price 5s.

Readings for a Month preparatory to Confirmation: Compiled from the Works of Writers of the Early and of the English Church. New *and cheaper* Edition. Fcp. 8vo. 4s.

Bowdler's Family Shakspeare: In which nothing is *added* to the Original Text; but those words and expressions are *omitted* which cannot with propriety be read aloud. Illustrated with Thirty-six Vignettes engraved on Wood from original Designs by

G. COOKE, R.A.	T. STOTHARD, R.A.
R. COOKE,	H. THOMSON, R.A.
H. HOWARD, R.A.	R. WESTALL, R.A.
H. SINGLETON,	R. WOODFORDE, R.A.
R. SMIRKE, R.A.	

New Edition, printed in a more convenient form. 6 vols. fcp. 8vo. price 30s. cloth; separately, 5s. each.

*** The LIBRARY EDITION, with the same Illustrations, in One Volume, medium 8vo. price 21s. cloth.

Sharp's New British Gazetteer, or Topographical Dictionary of the British Islands and Narrow Seas: Comprising concise Descriptions of about Sixty Thousand Places, Seats, Natural Features, and Objects of Note, founded on the best authorities. 2 vols. 8vo. price £2. 16s.

"We have already had occasion to mention this book, and a careful examination of its contents has convinced us of its great value. The remarkable clearness with which its condensations and abbreviations are made appears to us its most admirable feature. We have no book of similar bulk in the language containing anything like the amount of information of various kinds so well arranged and so easily accessible as in this new gazetteer. Every article bears the mark of studied, careful, and exact compilation. It comprehends both the topography and the hydrography of the United Kingdom, and is constructed on the plan of facilitating reference by bringing together as many articles as possible under distinct heads.... All the positions have been retaken from the maps; and not only the county but the quarter of the county given in which a name might be looked for. We must, in short, repeat with a liberal acquiescence what Mr. Sharp himself remarks of his five years' diligent labour, that it will be found to comprise, in a clear and legible type, more substantial information, collected from original sources, and put into a convenient form, than the bulkiest of its class." EXAMINER.

Short Whist; its Rise, Progress, and Laws: With Observations to make any one a Whist-Player. Containing also the Laws of Piquet, Cassino, Ecarté, Cribbage, Backgammon. By Major A. New Edition; to which are added, Precepts for Tyros, by Mrs. B. Fcp. 8vo. 3s.

Sinclair.—The Journey of Life. By CATHERINE SINCLAIR, Author of *The Business of Life.* New Edition. Fcp. 8vo. 5s.

Sir Roger De Coverley. From the Spectator. With Notes and Illustrations, by W. HENRY WILLS; and 12 Wood Engravings from Designs by F. TAYLER. Second *and cheaper* Edition. Crown 8vo. 10s. 6d.; or 21s. in morocco by Hayday.—An Edition without Woodcuts, in 16mo. price 1s.

The Sketches: Three Tales. By the Authors of *Amy Herbert, The Old Man's Home,* and *Hawkstone.* The *Third Edition;* with 6 Illustrations in Aquatint. Fcp. 8vo. price 4s. 6d. boards.

Smee's Elements of Electro-Metallurgy. Third Edition, revised, corrected, and considerably enlarged; with Electrotypes and numerous Woodcuts. Post 8vo. 10s. 6d.

Smith (G.)—History of Wesleyan Methodism: VOL. I. Wesley and his Times. By GEORGE SMITH, F.A.S., Member of the Royal Asiatic Society, &c.; Author of *Sacred Annals, or Researches into the History and Religion of Mankind,* &c. Crown 8vo. with 8 Facsimiles of Methodist Society Tickets, price 10s. 6d. cloth.

Smith (G. V.)—The Prophecies relating to Nineveh and the Assyrians. Translated from the Hebrew, with Historical Introductions and Notes, exhibiting the principal Results of the recent Discoveries. By GEORGE VANCE SMITH, B.A. Post 8vo. with a Map, price 10s. 6d. cloth.

Smith (J.)—The Voyage and Shipwreck of St. Paul: With Dissertations on the Life and Writings of St. Luke, and the Ships and Navigation of the Ancients. By JAMES SMITH, of Jordanhill, Esq., F.R.S. *Second Edition*; with Charts, Views, and Woodcuts. Crown 8vo. 8s. 6d.

A Memoir of the Rev. Sydney Smith. By his Daughter, LADY HOLLAND. With a Selection from his Letters, edited by MRS. AUSTIN. *New Edition.* 2 vols. 8vo. 28s.

The Rev. Sydney Smith's Miscellaneous Works: Including his Contributions to The Edinburgh Review. Three Editions:—

1. A LIBRARY EDITION (the *Fourth*), in 3 vols. 8vo. with Portrait, 36s.
2. Complete in ONE VOLUME, with Portrait and Vignette. Square crown 8vo. price 21s. cloth; or 30s. bound in calf.
3. Another NEW EDITION, in 3 vols. fcp. 8vo. price 21s.

The Rev. Sydney Smith's Elementary Sketches of Moral Philosophy, delivered at the Royal Institution in the Years 1804, 1805, and 1806. Third Edition. Fcp. 8vo. 7s.

Snow.—A Two-Years' Cruise off Tierra del Fuego, the Falkland Islands, Patagonia, and the River Plate. A Narrative of Life in the Southern Seas. By W. PARKER SNOW, late Commander of the Mission Yacht *Allen Gardiner*; Author of "Voyage of the *Prince Albert* in Search of Sir John Franklin." With 3 coloured Charts and 6 tinted Illustrations. 2 vols. post 8vo. 24s.

"A Robinson-Crusoe style of narration, and a kind of rough and picturesque treatment, sustain the interest of the nautical descriptions more than might be supposed, the wild and violent weather of the Falkland Islands, with the dangers of their navigation and the peculiar character of the River Plate, have a novelty beyond the common run of voyaging. The adventures in Tierra del Fuego are very interesting." SPECTATOR.

Robert Southey's Complete Poetical Works; containing all the Author's last Introductions and Notes. The *Library Edition*, complete in One Volume, with Portrait and Vignette. Medium 8vo. price 21s. cloth; 42s. bound in morocco.—Also, the *First collected Edition*, in 10 vols. fcp. 8vo. with Portrait and 19 Vignettes, price 35s.

Select Works of the British Poets; from Chaucer to Lovelace inclusive. With Biographical Sketches by the late ROBERT SOUTHEY. Medium 8vo. price 30s.

Southey's Correspondence.—Selections from the Letters of Robert Southey, &c. Edited by his Son-in-Law, the Rev. JOHN WOOD WARTER, B.D., Vicar of West Tarring, Sussex. 4 vols. post 8vo. price 42s.

The Life and Correspondence of the late Robert Southey. Edited by his Son, the Rev. C. C. SOUTHEY, M.A., Vicar of Ardleigh. With Portraits and Landscape Illustrations. 6 vols. post 8vo. price 63s.

Southey's Doctor, complete in One Volume. Edited by the Rev. J. W. WARTER, B.D. With Portrait, Vignette, Bust, and coloured Plate. Square crown 8vo. 21s.

Southey's Commonplace-Books, complete in Four Volumes. Edited by the Rev. J. W. WARTER, B.D. 4 vols. square crown 8vo. price £3. 18s.

Each *Commonplace-Book*, complete in itself, may be had separately, as follows:—

FIRST SERIES—CHOICE PASSAGES, &c. 18s.
SECOND SERIES—SPECIAL COLLECTIONS. 18s.
THIRD SERIES—ANALYTICAL READINGS. 21s.
FOURTH SERIES—ORIGINAL MEMORANDA, &c. 21s.

Southey's Life of Wesley; and Rise and Progress of Methodism. New Edition, with Notes and Additions. Edited by the Rev. C. C. SOUTHEY, M.A. 2 vols. 8vo. with 2 Portraits, price 28s.

Spottiswoode.—A Tarantasse Journey through Eastern Russia, in the Autumn of 1856. By WILLIAM SPOTTISWOODE, M.A., F.R.S. With a Map of Russia, several Wood Engravings, and Seven Illustrations in tinted Lithography from Sketches by the Author. Post 8vo. price 10s. 6d.

Stephen.—Lectures on the History of France. By the Right Hon. SIR JAMES STEPHEN, K.C.B., LL.D., Professor of Modern History in the University of Cambridge. Third Edition. 2 vols. 8vo. price 24s.

Stephen.—Essays in Ecclesiastical Biography; from The Edinburgh Review. By the Right Hon. SIR JAMES STEPHEN, K.C.B., LL.D., Professor of Modern History in the University of Cambridge. Third Edition. 2 vols. 8vo. 24s.

Stonehenge.—The Greyhound: Being a Treatise on the Art of Breeding, Rearing, and Training Greyhounds for Public Running; their Diseases and Treatment: Containing also Rules for the Management of Coursing Meetings, and for the Decision of Courses. By STONEHENGE. With Frontispiece and Woodcuts. Square crown 8vo. price 21s. half-bound.

Stow. — The Training System, Moral Training School, and Normal Seminary for preparing Schoolmasters and Governesses. By DAVID STOW, Esq., Honorary Secretary to the Glasgow Normal Free Seminary. Tenth Edition; with Plates and Woodcuts. Post 8vo. price 6s.

Strickland. — Lives of the Queens of England. By AGNES STRICKLAND. Dedicated, by express permission, to Her Majesty. Embellished with Portraits of every Queen, engraved from the most authentic sources. Complete in 8 vols. post 8vo. price 7s. 6d. each. — Any Volume may be had *separately* to complete Sets.

Memoirs of Rear-Admiral Sir William Symonds, Knt., C.B., F.R.S., late Surveyor of the Navy. Published with the sanction of his Executors, as directed by his Will; and edited by J. A. SHARP. 8vo. with Plates and Wood Engravings.
[*In the press.*

Taylor. — Loyola: and Jesuitism in its Rudiments. By ISAAC TAYLOR. Post 8vo. price 10s. 6d.

Taylor. — Wesley and Methodism. By ISAAC TAYLOR. Post 8vo. Portrait, 10s. 6d.

Thacker's Courser's Annual Remembrancer and Stud-Book: Being an Alphabetical Return of the Running at all the Public Coursing Clubs in England, Ireland, and Scotland, for the Season 1856-57; with the *Pedigrees* (as far as received) of the DOGS. By ROBERT ABRAM WELSH, Liverpool. 8vo. 21s.

*** Published annually in *October*.

Thirlwall. — The History of Greece. By the Right Rev. the LORD BISHOP of ST. DAVID'S (the Rev. Connop Thirlwall). An improved Library Edition; with Maps. 8 vols. 8vo. price £3. — An Edition in 8 vols. fcp. 8vo. with Vignette Titles, price 28s.

Thomas. — Historical Notes relative to the History of England; embracing the Period from the Accession of King Henry VIII. to the Death of Queen Anne inclusive (1509 to 1714): Designed as a Book of instant Reference for the purpose of ascertaining the Dates of Events mentioned in History and in Manuscripts. The Names of Persons and Events mentioned in History within the above period placed in Alphabetical and Chronological Order, with Dates; and the Authority from whence taken given in each case, whether from Printed History or from Manuscripts. By F. S. THOMAS, Secretary of the Public Record Department. 3 vols. royal 8vo. price £2.

Thomson's Seasons. Edited by Bolton CORNEY, Esq. Illustrated with 77 fine Wood Engravings from Designs by Members of the Etching Club. Square crown 8vo. 21s. cloth; or 36s. bound in morocco.

Thomson (the Rev. Dr.) — An Outline of the necessary Laws of Thought: A Treatise on Pure and Applied Logic. By WILLIAM THOMSON, D.D., Provost of Queen's College, Oxford. *Fourth Edition*, carefully revised. Fcp. 8vo. price 7s. 6d.

Thomson's Tables of Interest, at Three, Four, Four-and-a-Half, and Five per Cent., from One Pound to Ten Thousand, and from 1 to 365 Days, in a regular progression of single Days; with Interest at all the above Rates, from One to Twelve Months, and from One to Ten Years. Also, numerous other Tables of Exchanges, Time, and Discounts. New Edition. 12mo. price 8s.

Thornbury. — Shakspeare's England; or, Sketches of Social History during the Reign of Elizabeth. By G. W. THORNBURY, Author of *History of the Buccaneers*, &c. 2 vols. crown 8vo. 21s.

"A work which stands unrivalled for the variety and entertaining character of its contents, and which well deserves a place on the library-shelf, by the side either of the historians of England or the prince of dramatists."
JOHN BULL.

The Thumb Bible; or, Verbum Sempiternum. By J. TAYLOR. Being an Epitome of the Old and New Testaments in English Verse. Reprinted from the Edition of 1693; bound and clasped. 64mo. 1s. 6d.

Bishop Tomline's Introduction to the Study of the Bible: Containing Proofs of the Authenticity and Inspiration of the Scriptures; a Summary of the History of the Jews; an Account of the Jewish Sects; and a brief Statement of Contents of several Books of the *Old Testament*. New Edition. Fcp. 8vo. 5s. 6d.

Tooke. — History of Prices, and of the State of the Circulation, during the Nine Years from 1848 to 1856 inclusive. Forming Vols. V. and VI. of Tooke's *History of Prices from* 1792 *to the Present Time*; and comprising a copious Index to the whole of the Six Volumes. By THOMAS TOOKE, F.R.S. and WILLIAM NEWMARCH. 2 vols. 8vo. price 52s. 6d.

Townsend. — Modern State Trials revised and illustrated with Essays and Notes. By W. C. TOWNSEND, Esq., M.A., Q.C. 2 vols. 8vo. price 30s.

COMPLETION OF THE TRAVELLER'S LIBRARY.

Summary of the Contents of the TRAVELLER'S LIBRARY, *now complete in* 10 Parts, *price One Shilling each, or in* 50 Volumes, *price* 2s. 6d. *each in cloth.*– *To be had also, in* complete Sets only, *at Five Guineas per Set, bound in clot. lettered, in* 25 Volumes, *classified as follows:*—

VOYAGES AND TRAVELS.

IN EUROPE.

A CONTINENTAL TOUR ....BY J. BARROW.
ARCTIC VOYAGES AND DISCOVERIES ...... BY F. MAYNE.
BRITTANY AND THE BIBLE ......BY I. HOPE.
BRITTANY AND THE CHASE ......BY I. HOPE.
CORSICA .... BY F. GREGOROVIUS.
GERMANY, ETC.: NOTES OF A TRAVELLER .... BY S. LAING.
ICELAND .... BY P. MILES.
NORWAY, A RESIDENCE IN ...... BY S. LAING.
NORWAY, RAMBLES IN ...... BY T. FORESTER.
RUSSIA .... BY THE MARQUIS DE CUSTINE.
RUSSIA AND TURKEY .. BY J. R. M'CULLOCH.
ST. PETERSBURG .... BY M. JERRMANN.
THE RUSSIANS OF THE SOUTH, BY S. BROOKS.
SWISS MEN AND SWISS MOUNTAINS BY R. FERGUSON.
MONT BLANC, ASCENT OF ......BY J. AULDJO.
SKETCHES OF NATURE IN THE ALPS .... BY F. VON TSCHUDI.
VISIT TO THE VAUDOIS OF PIEDMONT ....BY E. BAINES.

IN ASIA.

CHINA AND THIBET .. .BY THE ABBE' HUC.
SYRIA AND PALESTINE .. .. "EÖTHEN."
THE PHILIPPINE ISLANDS, BY P. GIRONIÈRE.

IN AFRICA.

AFRICAN WANDERINGS .. BY M. WERNE.
MOROCCO BY X. DURRIEU.
NIGER EXPLORATION BY T. J. HUTCHINSON.
THE ZULUS OF NATAL BY G. H. MASON.

IN AMERICA.

BRAZIL ....BY E. WILBERFORCE.
CANADA.. .. .. BY A. M. JAMESON.
CUBA BY W. H. HURLBUT.
NORTH AMERICAN WILDS ... BY C. LANMAN.

IN AUSTRALIA.

AUSTRALIAN COLONIES .. BY W. HUGHES.

ROUND THE WORLD.

A LADY'S VOYAGE... ... BY IDA PFEIFFER.

HISTORY AND BIOGRAPHY.

MEMOIR OF THE DUKE OF WELLINGTON.
THE LIFE OF MARSHAL TURENNE........ BY THE REV. T. O. COCKAYNE.
SCHAMYL .... BY BODENSTEDT AND WAGNER.
FERDINAND I. AND MAXIMILIAN II. .... BY RANKE.
FRANCIS ARAGO'S AUTOBIOGRAPHY.
THOMAS HOLCROFT'S MEMOIRS.
CHESTERFIELD & SELWYN, BY A. HAYWARD.
SWIFT AND RICHARDSON, BY LORD JEFFREY.
DEFOE AND CHURCHILL BY J. FORSTER.
ANECDOTES OF DR JOHNSON, BY MRS PIOZZI.
TURKEY AND CHRISTENDOM.
LEIPSIC CAMPAIGN, BY THE REV G. R. GLEIG.
AN ESSAY ON THE LIFE AND GENIUS OF THOMAS FULLER BY HENRY ROGERS.

ESSAYS BY LORD MACAULAY.

WARREN HASTINGS.
LORD CLIVE.
WILLIAM PITT.
THE EARL OF CHATHAM.
RANKE'S HISTORY OF THE POPES.
GLADSTONE ON CHURCH AND STATE.
ADDISON'S LIFE AND WRITINGS.
HORACE WALPOLE.
LORD BACON.
LORD BYRON.
COMIC DRAMATISTS OF THE RESTORATION.
FREDERIC THE GREAT.
HALLAM'S CONSTITUTIONAL HISTORY.
CROKER'S EDITION OF BOSWELL'S LIFE OF JOHNSON.

LORD MACAULAY'S SPEECHES ON PARLIAMENTARY REFORM.

WORKS OF FICTION.

THE LOVE STORY, FROM SOUTHEY'S *DOCTOR.*
SIR ROGER DE COVERLEY.... FROM THE *SPECTATOR.*
MEMOIRS OF A MAITRE-D'ARMES, BY DUMAS.
CONFESSIONS OF A WORKING MAN .. ..BY E. SOUVESTRE.
AN ATTIC PHILOSOPHER IN PARIS .. ..BY E. SOUVESTRE.
SIR EDWARD SEAWARD'S NARRATIVE OF HIS SHIPWRECK.

NATURAL HISTORY, &c.

NATURAL HISTORY OF CREATION .... BY DR. L. KEMP.
INDICATIONS OF INSTINCT, BY DR. L. KEMP.
ELECTRIC TELEGRAPH, &c. BY DR G. WILSON.
OUR COAL-FIELDS AND OUR COAL-PITS.
CORNWALL, ITS MINES, MINERS, &c.

MISCELLANEOUS WORKS.

LECTURES AND ADDRESSES BY THE EARL OF CARLISLE.
SELECTIONS FROM SYDNEY SMITH'S WRITINGS.
PRINTING ....BY A. STARK.
RAILWAY MORALS AND RAILWAY POLICY . BY H. SPENCER.
MORMONISM.. BY THE REV W. J. CONYBEARE.
LONDON .... BY J. R. M'CULLOCH.

The Traveller's Library being now complete, the Publishers call attention to this collection as well adapted for *Travellers* and *Emigrants*, for *School-room Libraries*, the *Libraries of Mechanics' Institutions, Young Men's Libraries*, the *Libraries of Ships*, and similar purposes. The separate volumes are suited for *School Prizes, Presents to Young People*, and for general instruction and entertainment. The Series comprises fourteen of the most popular of Lord Macaulay's *Essays*, and his *Speeches* on Parliamentary Reform. The department of Travels contains some account of eight of the principal countries of Europe, as well as travels in four districts of Africa, in four of America, and in three of Asia. Madame Pfeiffer's *First Journey round the World* is included; and a general account of the *Australian Colonies*. In Biography and History will be found Lord Macaulay's Biographical Sketches of *Warren Hastings, Clive, Pitt, Walpole, Bacon*, and others; besides Memoirs of *Wellington, Turenne, F. Arago*, &c.; an Essay on the Life and Genius of *Thomas Fuller*, with Selections from his Writings, by Mr. Henry Rogers; and a history of the *Leipsic Campaign*, by Mr. Gleig,—which is the only separate account of this remarkable campaign. Works of Fiction did not come within the plan of the TRAVELLER'S LIBRARY; but the *Confessions of a Working Man*, by Souvestre, which is indeed a fiction founded on fact, has been included, and has been read with unusual interest by many of the working classes, for whose use it is especially recommended. Dumas's story of the *Maitre-d'Armes*, though in form a work of fiction, gives a striking picture of an episode in the history of Russia. Amongst the works on Science and Natural Philosophy, a general view of Creation is embodied in Dr. Kemp's *Natural History of Creation*; and in his *Indications of Instinct* remarkable facts in natural history are collected. Dr. Wilson has contributed a popular account of the *Electric Telegraph*. In the volumes on the *Coal-Fields*, and on the Tin and other Mining Districts of *Cornwall*, is given an account of the mineral wealth of England, the habits and manners of the miners, and the scenery of the surrounding country. It only remains to add, that among the Miscellaneous Works are a Selection of the best Writings of the Rev. Sydney Smith; Lord Carlisle's *Lectures and Addresses*; an account of *Mormonism*, by the Rev. W. J. Conybeare; an exposition of *Railway* management and mismanagement, by Mr. Herbert Spencer; an account of the Origin and Practice of *Printing*, by Mr. Stark; and an account of *London*, by Mr. M'Culloch.

"If we were called upon to lay the first stone of a Mechanics' Institute or Book-Society's Collection, it should be composed of the hundred and two parts of the *Traveller's Library*. It is the best Shilling Series extant. Here are Mr. Macaulay's best writings, the anthologia of Sydney Smith, some admirable literary essays by different authors, several excellent volumes of science, narratives of travel in eight European, four American, four African, and three Asiatic countries, and examples from the works of Souvestre and Dumas. Bound together, they form twenty-five convenient volumes, which any society of a hundred and five members may possess, upon payment of one shilling each. An association of this kind, formed in every small town, would thus create sufficient basis for a free library upon a modest scale. Good books are *not* beyond the reach of working men, if working men will combine to obtain them." LEADER.

☞ The *Traveller's Library* may also be had as originally issued in 102 parts, 1s. each, forming 50 vols. 2s. 6d. each; or any separate parts or volumes.

Trollope.—Barchester Towers. By ANTHONY TROLLOPE. 3 vols. post 8vo. price 31s. 6d.

"*Barchester Towers* (a kind of sequel in continuation of Mr. Trollope's former novel *The Warden*) does not depend only on story for its interest; the careful writing, the good humour with a tendency often to be Shandean in its expression, and the sense and right feeling with which the way is threaded among questions of high church and low church, are very noticeable, and secure for it unquestionable rank among the few really well-written tales that every season produces." EXAMINER.

Trollope.—The Warden. By Anthony Trollope. Post 8vo. 10s. 6d.

Sharon Turner's Sacred History of the World, attempted to be Philosophically considered, in a Series of Letters to a Son. New Edition, edited by the Rev. S. TURNER. 3 vols. post 8vo. price 31s. 6d.

Sharon Turner's History of England during the Middle Ages: Comprising the Reigns from the Norman Conquest to the Accession of Henry VIII. Fifth Edition, revised by the Rev. S. TURNER. 4 vols. 8vo. price 50s.

Sharon Turner's History of the Anglo-Saxons, from the Earliest Period to the Norman Conquest. Seventh Edition, revised by the Rev. S. TURNER. 3 vols. 8vo. 36s.

Dr. Turton's Manual of the Land and Fresh-Water Shells of Great Britain. New Edition, thoroughly revised and brought up to the Present Time. Edited by Dr. J. E. GRAY, F.R.S., &c., Keeper of the Zoological Department in the British Museum. Crown 8vo. with Coloured Plates. [*In the press.*

Dr. Ure's Dictionary of Arts, Manufactures, and Mines: Containing a clear Exposition of their Principles and Practice. Fourth Edition, much enlarged; most of the Articles being entirely re-written, and many new Articles added. With nearly 1,600 Woodcuts. 2 vols. 8vo. price 60s.

Van Der Hoeven's Handbook of Zoology. Translated from the Second Dutch Edition by the Rev. WILLIAM CLARK, M.D., F.R.S., &c., late Fellow of Trinity College, and Professor of Anatomy in the University of Cambridge; with additional References furnished by the Author. In Two Volumes. Vol. I. *Invertebrate Animals*; with 15 Plates, comprising numerous Figures. 8vo. 30s.

Vehse.—Memoirs of the Court, Aristocracy, and Diplomacy of Austria. By Dr. E. VEHSE. Translated from the German by FRANZ DEMMLER. 2 vols. post 8vo. 21s.

Von Tempsky.—Mitla: A Narrative of Incidents and Personal Adventures on a Journey in Mexico and Guatemala in the Years 1853 and 1854: With Observations on the Modes of Life in those Countries. By G. F. VON TEMPSKY. Edited by J. S. BELL, Author of *Journal of a Residence in Circassia in the Years* 1836 *to* 1839. With Illustrations in Chromolithography and Engravings on Wood. 8vo. [*In the press.*

Wade.—England's Greatness: Its Rise and Progress in Government, Laws, Religion, and Social Life; Agriculture, Commerce, and Manufactures; Science, Literature, and the Arts, from the Earliest Period to the Peace of Paris. By JOHN WADE, Author of the *Cabinet Lawyer*, &c. Post 8vo. 10s. 6d.

Waterton.—Essays on Natural History, chiefly Ornithology. By C. WATERTON, Esq. With an Autobiography of the Author, and Views of Walton Hall. New and cheaper Edition. 2 vols. fcp. 8vo. price 10s.

Waterton's Essays on Natural History. Third Series; with a Continuation of the Autobiography, and a Portrait of the Author. Fcp 8vo. price 6s.

Webster and Parkes's Encyclopædia of Domestic Economy; comprising such subjects as are most immediately connected with Housekeeping: As, The Construction of Domestic Edifices, with the Modes of Warming, Ventilating, and Lighting them—A description of the various articles of Furniture, with the nature of their Materials—Duties of Servants—&c. New Edition; with nearly 1,000 Woodcuts. 8vo. price 50s.

Weld.—Vacations in Ireland. By CHARLES RICHARD WELD, Barrister-at-Law. Post 8vo. with a tinted View of Birr Castle, price 10s. 6d.

Weld.—A Vacation Tour in the United States and Canada. By C. R. WELD, Barrister-at-Law. Post 8vo. with Map, 10s. 6d.

West.—Lectures on the Diseases of Infancy and Childhood. By CHARLES WEST, M.D., Physician to the Hospital for Sick Children; Physician-Accoucheur to, and Lecturer on Midwifery at, St. Bartholomew's Hospital. Third Edition. 8vo. 14s.

Willich's Popular Tables for ascertaining the Value of Lifehold, Leasehold, and Church Property, Renewal Fines, &c. With numerous additional Tables—Chemical, Astronomical, Trigonometrical, Common and Hyperbolic Logarithms; Constants, Squares, Cubes, Roots, Reciprocals, &c. Fourth Edition, enlarged. Post 8vo. price 10s.

Whitelocke's Journal of the English Embassy to the Court of Sweden in the Years 1653 and 1654. A New Edition, revised by HENRY REEVE, Esq., F.S.A. 2 vols. 8vo. 24s.

Wilmot's Abridgment of Blackstone's Commentaries on the Laws of England, intended for the use of Young Persons, and comprised in a series of Letters from a Father to his Daughter. 12mo. price 6s. 6d.

Wilson (W.)—Bryologia Britannica: Containing the Mosses of Great Britain and Ireland systematically arranged and described according to the Method of *Bruch* and *Schimper;* with 61 illustrative Plates. Being a New Edition, enlarged and altered, of the *Muscologia Britannica* of Messrs. Hooker and Taylor. By WILLIAM WILSON, President of the Warrington Natural History Society. 8vo. 42s.; or, with the Plates coloured, price £4. 4s. cloth.

Yonge.—A New English-Greek Lexicon: Containing all the Greek Words used by Writers of good authority. By C. D. YONGE, B.A. *Second Edition*, revised and corrected. Post 4to. price 21s.

Yonge's New Latin Gradus: Containing Every Word used by the Poets of good authority. For the use of Eton, Westminster, Winchester, Harrow, Charterhouse, and Rugby Schools; King's College, London; and Marlborough College. *Fifth Edition.* Post 8vo. price 9s.; or with APPENDIX of *Epithets* classified according to their *English* Meaning, 12s.

Youatt.—The Horse. By William Youatt. With a Treatise of Draught. New Edition, with numerous Wood Engravings, from Designs by William Harvey. (Messrs. LONGMAN and Co.'s Edition should be ordered.) 8vo. price 10s.

Youatt.—The Dog. By William Youatt. A New Edition; with numerous Engravings, from Designs by W. Harvey. 8vo. 6s.

Young.—The Christ of History: An Argument grounded in the Facts of His Life on Earth. By JOHN YOUNG, LL.D. Second Edition. Post 8vo. 7s. 6d.

Young.—The Mystery; or, Evil and God. By JOHN YOUNG, LL.D. Post 8vo. 7s. 6d.

Zumpt's Grammar of the Latin Language. Translated and adapted for the use of English Students by DR. L. SCHMITZ, F.R.S.E.: With numerous Additions and Corrections by the Author and Translator. 4th Edition, thoroughly revised. 8vo. 14s.

[*October* 1857.

PRINTED BY SPOTTISWOODE AND CO., NEW-STREET SQUARE, LONDON.